The Teaching
podcast

Praise for

Practicing the Way

"In this spacious, eminently readable volume, John Mark Comer meditates on how Christian discipleship is, at its root, the radical task of becoming an apprentice of Jesus—to be with him, to become like him, and to do as he did. The deceptively simple call is to take Jesus at his word, to open ourselves fully to him, to organize our schedules, our routines, our study, our daily practices around him, and, by doing so, to become people who can do as he would in our day and our culture. Comer's experiences as a pastor, teacher, thinker, and an apprentice himself are helpfully on display here. Sit with this book slowly and let it be your guide into a life of apprenticeship to Jesus."
—Tish Harrison Warren, Anglican priest and author of *Liturgy of the Ordinary* and *Prayer in the Night*

"I love John Mark Comer's vision for life—to be with Jesus, become more like him, and aspire to do what Jesus would do. This book can help us all in our own walk with Jesus."
—Nicky Gumbel, pioneer of Alpha

"In *Practicing the Way*, John Mark Comer brilliantly shows us what it means to follow Jesus, and here is the best part: As you read, you will want nothing more than to be on Jesus' heels. We are a disciple-less generation, and yet, walking this closely with Jesus is our way back to the purpose of life. This is one of the most important books I have read in a decade, and if we would all follow in this way, our lives would change and the world would change."
—Jennie Allen, *New York Times* bestselling author of *Get Out of Your Head* and *Find Your People* and founder and visionary of IF:Gathering

"In *Practicing the Way*, John Mark Comer offers us a portrait of following Jesus that is as profound and compelling as it is simple. Be prepared to take an honest look at your own life habits and prayerfully ask, *What kind of person am I becoming* and *Is it more like Jesus or less?* Here you will find a beautiful picture of the kind of life Jesus envisioned for his followers and a practical pathway to experience it for yourself."
—Tim Mackie, co-founder of BibleProject

"This is the book that I want everyone in my church to read. It is an invitation deeper for the lifelong follower of Jesus, and the perfect primer for the new believer. Somehow, in a way only John Mark can do, he has plunged the depths of the gospel invitation in a way that is relatable, accessible, and readable for the everyday seeker."
—Tyler Staton, lead pastor of Bridgetown Church

"This book presents Jesus as not merely someone we interpret but as a timeless teacher who interprets us. Our world of imminent distractions and luring cultural traps robs us of a basic soul satisfaction. In what is sure to be a classic, John Mark Comer takes us back to the future. Learning from the desert fathers but spoken like a timely sage, John Mark explains the abundant life to a generation divested of its virtue and void of its principle. Herein is a window to the meaning and significance of life that only Jesus affords. John Mark has given us the antidote to failed religion and generational hypocrisy. Read it slowly. Be changed deeply."
—Rev. Dr. Charlie Dates, senior pastor of Salem Baptist Church of Chicago and Progressive Baptist Church, Chicago

Also by John Mark Comer

My Name is Hope

Loveology

Garden City

God Has a Name

The Ruthless Elimination of Hurry

Live No Lies

Practicing the Way

Practicing
the Way

Be with Jesus

Become like him

Do as he did

John Mark
Comer

WATERBROOK

Italics in Scripture quotations reflect the author's added emphasis.

Details in some anecdotes and stories have been changed to protect the
identities of the persons involved.

Copyright © 2024 by John Mark Comer

All rights reserved.

Published in the United States by WaterBrook, an imprint of Random
House, a division of Penguin Random House LLC.

WATERBROOK and colophon are registered trademarks of Penguin Random
House LLC.

Published in association with Yates & Yates, www.yates2.com.

Library of Congress Cataloging-in-Publication Data
Names: Comer, John Mark, author.
Title: Practicing the way : be with Jesus, become like him, do as he did /
    John Mark Comer.
Description: Colorado Springs : WaterBrook, [2024] | Includes
    bibliographical references.
Identifiers: LCCN 2023028627 | ISBN 9780593193822 (hardcover) |
    ISBN 9780593193839 (ebook)
Subjects: LCSH: Jesus Christ—Person and offices. | Christian life—Biblical
    teaching.
Classification: LCC BT203 .C645 2024 | DDC 232—dc23/
    eng/20230907
LC record available at https://lccn.loc.gov/2023028627

Printed in the United States of America on acid-free paper.

waterbrookmultnomah.com

9 8 7 6 5 4 3

First Edition

Book design by Ryan Wesley Peterson

Most WaterBrook books are available at special quantity discounts for
bulk purchase for premiums, fundraising, and corporate and educational
needs by organizations, churches, and businesses. Special books or book
excerpts also can be created to fit specific needs. For details, contact
specialmarketscms@penguinrandomhouse.com.

"Come, follow me."

——Jesus, Mark 1v17

"May you be covered in the dust of your rabbi."
—first-century Jewish blessing

Dust

Who are you following?

Everybody is following *somebody*—or at least something.

Put another way, we're all disciples.

The question isn't, Am I a disciple?

It's, *Who* or *what* am I a disciple *of*?

I know, I know; what I just said is akin to heresy in the modern world. We want *so* badly to believe that we—and we alone— plot our course, captain our ship, control our destiny. We aspire to lead, not to follow.

But, question: How is that working out for you?

Do you ever feel that nagging "thought" tug at the back of your mind: *Is the life I'm living the life I most deeply desire? Is this it?*

I was born and raised on the West Coast of America. It's an open secret that the US in general and my home state of California in particular are built on what sociologists call "the myth of the rugged individual." Dr. Robert Bellah called it "radical individual- ism" and said it's the defining trait of America.[1]

And yet "no man is an island," as the poet John Donne once said.[2] And no woman is either. In the words of the *New York Times* columnist Tish Harrison Warren, "None of us comes to what we believe by ourselves. *The world has no free thinkers.*"[3]

(You see, I'm not the only cultural heretic around . . .)

Powerful forces have a vested interest in our believing the myth (and it *is* a myth) that we are following no one at all. Many of the cultural liturgies that indoctrinate us daily—"Be true to yourself," "You do you," "Speak your truth"—can be traced back to sources with a nefarious agenda.[4] If "they" (whether multinational corporations, politicians, anti-democratic government agents, marketing departments, influencers who just want more followers, etc., etc.) can make us believe that each person is a blank slate, just following the inner compass of our "authentic self" in an upward march to happiness, then they can keep us blind to all the ways we've been "discipled"—formed and manipulated—by *their* desires.

Any skilled con artist knows the key to deceiving your mark is to get them to believe your scheme was *their* idea. Translation: The key to getting people to follow you is to convince them they aren't following anyone at all.

With the rise of social media empires and their spooky digital algorithms, these powerful forces now have direct access to our flows of consciousness every time we slide our thumbs across our phones. What we are led to believe are just ads, news links, retweets, and random digital flotsam are, in reality, mass behavior modification techniques intentionally designed to influence how we think, feel, believe, shop, vote, and live. To quote the tech philosopher Jaron Lanier, "What might once have been called advertising must now be understood as continuous behavior modification on a titanic scale."[5] The "world" (as it's called in the New Testament) is *forming* us, constantly.

But what is it forming us *into*?

Because we are each becoming something. That's the crux of the human experience: the process of becoming a person. To be human is to change. To grow. To evolve. This is by God's design.

The question is not, Am I becoming a person?

It's, *Who* or *what* am I becoming?

If you plot the trajectory of your life over the next five decades and envision yourself at seventy, eighty, or a hundred, what kind of person do you see on the horizon? Does the projection in your mind fill you with hope? Or dread?

For those of us who desire to follow Jesus, here is the reality we must turn and face: If we're not being intentionally formed by Jesus himself, then it's highly likely we are being unintentionally formed by someone or something *else*.[6]

So, again, Who are you following?

The deeper question here is, In whom are you *trusting*? Who (or what) do you put your faith in to show you the way to the life you desire? It's my conviction that contrary to what we hear, living by faith isn't a Christian thing or even a religious thing; it's a *human* thing—we *all* live by faith.

The question isn't, Am I going to believe?

It's, *Who* or *what* am I going to believe *in*?

Meaning, Who or what am I going to *entrust* my life to? Do I really want to trust *myself*—or any other human, for that matter?

We creatures who seem to have gotten ourselves into the very mess we're trying to fix?

It's only human to be drawn to someone—a celebrity or guru or historical figure—and to desire to become like them. This is part of how God wired us to grow. We all have an ideal life we aspire to, and when we find a person or idea system that seems to embody what we want, we "follow" them, we put our trust in them. Or, in more Christian language, we "believe."

Who do you believe in?[7] Who is your luminary of choice, the person whose orbit you would give anything to spend a few days living in?

Put another way, Who is your rabbi?

I am one of many people who have found Jesus of Nazareth to be the most radiant light to ever grace the human scene. I'm an avid reader, and through the gift of literature, I have peered inside the minds of some of history's greatest thinkers. All of them have laudable traits (and some not so laudable ones too). But the longer I live and learn, the more I'm convinced that Jesus has no real competition, ancient or modern. In my estimation, no other thinker, philosopher, leader, philosophy, or ideology has the coherence, sophistication, and deep inner resonance of Jesus and his Way. Much less the staggering *beauty*.

In our secular age, the air we breathe is filled with skepticism, ennui, distrust of all authority, and the bending of truth to desire and feeling. Inside this cultural atmosphere, we are *all* doubting Thomas.

But even on the days when I struggle to believe that Jesus was who he claimed to be (spoiler: more than just a rabbi), I *want* to believe. I *want* Jesus' vision of life in the kingdom of God to be true. I resonate at a soul level with the disciple Peter's conclusion:

> Lord, to whom shall we go? You have the words of eternal life.[8]

I stand (or really, walk) with a vast multitude of others around the world and down through history who have come to believe: *There simply is no better way, truth, or life to be found than that of Jesus.*

Of the myriad of options, he's the one I choose to follow. I'm going to end up following someone, so I choose to follow Jesus.

The philosopher Dallas Willard used to say, "There is no problem in human life that apprenticeship to Jesus cannot solve." Following or, as I will describe it in the pages to come, *apprenticing* Jesus, is the solution to the problem of the so-called human condition. Name your malaise: political polarization, climate change, looming global war, the mental health epidemic, addiction, Christian nationalism, widespread hypocrisy among Christian leaders, our simple inability to be kind . . .

There is no problem in human life that apprenticeship to Jesus cannot solve.

You may have picked up this book because you're seriously considering becoming a follower of Jesus, but you want to know what it is you're saying yes to. That's wise; Jesus urged potential followers to "count the cost" before becoming his disciples.[9]

Or you may already be a Christian but find in your heart a growing desire to take your faith more seriously—to become an apprentice of Jesus. To add a new level of intentionality to your spiritual formation. To live on purpose, not on accident.

yes Or you may be a longtime follower of Jesus but feel like you've hit a plateau. You're stuck, and you ache to get unstuck, to experience a deeper level of healing. To close the gap between your life and Jesus' "life that is truly life."[10] In other words, you want to become a saint.

Whoever you are and whatever prompted you to read this book, welcome. I'm so happy you've come along.

I am a follower of Jesus who has spent the better part of my adult life working out discipleship to Jesus in the post-Christian West. I have come to believe that there is a Way of life laid down by Jesus himself, and that if we give ourselves to it—and ultimately to *him*—it will lead to the life we *all* most truly crave.

This book is the culmination of decades of experience, trial and error, more failures than successes, and a lot of lessons learned in the school of hard knocks. But the pages to come are no tome; they are simply an exploration and explanation of what I believe to be three of the most important words ever spoken in the long annals of human history:

Come, follow me.[11]

Contrary to what many assume, Jesus did not invite people to convert to Christianity. He didn't even call people to become Christians (keep reading . . .); he invited people to apprentice under him into a whole new way of living. To be transformed.

My thesis is simple: Transformation *is* possible *if* we are willing to arrange our lives around the practices, rhythms, and truths that Jesus himself did, which will open our lives to God's power to change. Said another way, we can be transformed *if* we are willing to apprentice ourselves to Jesus.

Then—and only then—can we become the people we ache to be and live the lives we were destined for.

That said, we hear the language of "following" Jesus all the time. But what exactly does it *mean*?

It means practicing the Way.

Practicing the Way—

Apprentice to Jesus

Imagine this: Your name is Simon. You're a first-century Hebrew, likely in your late teens or early twenties. You run a fishing business in the Galilee, a string of villages in the north of Israel. Your life is pretty much mapped out for you. You do what your father did, and his father before him. Living under Roman occupation, there aren't a lot of options. Keep your head down, be quiet, pay your taxes.

One day you're waist deep in water, casting your net alongside your brother, Andrew, when you notice a man walking toward you on the beach. You instantly recognize his face. It's him: *Jesus,* from Nazareth, just a few miles away. Everyone is talking about this man—he is saying and doing things no rabbi has said or done. Ever.

Here he is, walking straight toward you. You make eye contact. His eyes sparkle like stars, like there's a cosmos behind them. He radiates joy, but there's no small talk:

> Come, follow me . . . and I will send you out to fish for people.[1]

You're absolutely stunned.

It can't be.

Not *you.*

You immediately drop your nets, drag Andrew out of the boat (though he doesn't need any coaxing), leave *everything* behind, and fall in step behind Jesus, elated to be in his company. Or in the words of the biographer Mark, "At once they left their nets and followed him."[2]

Now, if you're familiar with this story, it's easy to miss how bizarre it is. What would make Simon literally walk away from a profitable business and leave behind his family and friends, with zero planning, all to follow a man with no income stream, no organization, and no official position into an unknown future? Is this drinking the Kool-Aid before there was Kool-Aid?

Or are we missing something?

Jesus was a rabbi

If you were Simon, and Jesus were to visit your synagogue one fine Sabbath morning to preach, the category you likely would have put him in was that of a rabbi, or teacher.

The title *rabbi* literally means "master."[3] Rabbis were the spiritual masters of Israel. Not only were they expert teachers of the Torah (the Scriptures of their day); they were also magnetic examples of life with God—those special few who shine with an inner luminescence.

Every rabbi had his "yoke"—a Hebrew idiom for his set of teachings, his way of reading Scripture, his take on how to thrive as a human being in God's good world. How you, too, could taste a little of what they'd tasted . . .

Rabbis came from a broad cross section of society. They could have been farmers or blacksmiths or even carpenters.[4] Most trained under another rabbi for many years, then began to teach and call their own disciples around the age of thirty. But there was no formal certification like in our modern educational system. Authority worked differently. Your *life* and *teaching* were your credentials.

Rabbis were itinerant, and most were unpaid. (Some worked their farms or ran businesses for seasons of the year, then traveled in the off-season.) They walked from town to town to teach in whatever synagogue would have them, relying on the hospitality of people of peace. They often spoke in parables and riddles. Normally, they traveled with a small band of disciples, teaching not in a classroom but in the open air and along the road—not from a textbook or curriculum but from the Torah and the school of life.[5]

Over and over again in the four Gospels, Jesus is addressed as "rabbi."[6]

But he was no ordinary rabbi.[7]

Everywhere he went, the crowds were "astonished" and "overwhelmed with wonder."[8] The biographer Luke wrote, "All spoke well of him and were amazed at the gracious words that came from his lips."[9] Mark said, "The people were amazed at his teaching, because he taught them as one who had authority, not as the teachers of the law."[10] They gave feedback like "Where did this man get this wisdom . . . ?" and even "No one ever spoke the way this man does."[11]

Of course, saying that Jesus was a rabbi is about as insightful as saying that he was Jewish (although that's another truth copious numbers of people forget). But sadly, very few people—*including many Christians*—take Jesus seriously as a spiritual teacher.

To some, he's a wraithlike apparition, there to inspire later generations to a fuzzy kind of goodwill. To others, he is a social revolutionary—RESIST!—fist up to the Roman Empire then and all empires now. To a large number of Western Christians, he is a delivery mechanism for a particular theory of atonement, as if the only reason he came was to die, not to live.

As a result, many Christians don't consider Jesus all that smart. Holy, sure. Kind, yes. Even divine. But intelligent? Not really.

An increasing number of Christians don't agree with him on crucial matters of human flourishing. They would rather trust a politician, celebrity, or pastor gone rogue than Jesus the teacher and the disciples who studied directly under him. They would never even think to consult Jesus on the pressing matters of our time: politics, racial justice, sexuality, gender, mental health, and so on. As Dallas Willard said, "What lies at the heart of the astonishing disregard of Jesus found in the moment-to-moment existence of multitudes of professing Christians is a simple *lack of respect for him.*"[12]

This is vital, because if to "follow" Jesus is to trust him to lead you to the life you desire, it's very hard (if not *impossible*) to entrust your life to someone you don't respect.

But what if Jesus was more intelligent than any other teacher in history? More than Stephen Hawking or Karl Marx or even the Buddha? What if he was a brilliant sage with insight into the human condition that is still, two millennia later, without parallel? What if he simply has no equal or peer?

Now, *that* could be someone to put your trust in.

Of course, to call Jesus a brilliant rabbi is not to say he was *just* a brilliant rabbi. The sign hanging above Jesus' head when he was crucified said KING OF THE JEWS, not GURU. It tells you a lot about Jesus that his enemies perceived him as a political threat.

This would have made perfect sense in Jesus' culture. Moses, the great historical luminary of the Jewish people, was called Moshe Rabbenu ("Moses Our Rabbi") and Israel's Great Teacher. First-century Israelites were waiting for a *new* Moses to appear and lead a *new* exodus out of the Roman Empire—a figure they began to call the Messiah. Some expected the long-awaited Messiah to appear as a warrior or military leader, but many expected him to come as a great teacher. As two scholars put it, "The Jewish people believed that becoming a great scholar of the Scriptures represented life's supreme achievement. In such a culture, it made sense that the Messiah should be the greatest of teachers. No wonder Jesus became a Jewish rabbi."[13]

But we Christians believe he was even *more* than the Messiah. Jesus made claims that no Jewish king would ever dare utter—claims that got him accused of blasphemy, a capital offense in his world. As one of his critics put it, "We are not stoning you for any good work . . . but for blasphemy, because you, a mere man, claim to be God."[14]

But to say Jesus was *more* than just a rabbi or even the Messiah is not to say he was anything *less* than a brilliant, provocative, wise, spiritual master of how to live and thrive in this our Father's world.

He was a rabbi. And like most rabbis of his day, Jesus had disciples . . .

Three goals of an apprentice

Contrary to popular opinion, Jesus did not invent discipleship. Rabbis with a small coterie of disciples were regularly seen walking around Galilee. Just a few years before Jesus, Rabbi Hillel called eighty disciples. Rabbi Akiva—a famous teacher a few decades after Jesus—had only five, but thousands were said to "follow" him around Israel. In the New Testament itself, John the Baptizer had disciples, as did the Pharisees; the apostle Paul was formerly a disciple of a nationally known rabbi named Gamaliel. Discipleship (or, as I'm about to relabel it, apprenticeship) was the pinnacle of the first-century Jewish educational system, much like a PhD or graduate program is in our system today.

That means to understand discipleship, we first must understand the Jewish educational system. (Don't worry; I promise to keep this short.)

Jewish kids started school around five years old at the local *bet sefer* ("the house of the book"), which was the equivalent of elementary school. Normally the *bet sefer* was built onto the side of the synagogue and run by a full-time scribe or teacher. The curriculum was the Torah, and in an oral culture, by the age twelve or thirteen, most kids would have the *entire* Torah—*Genesis, Exodus, Leviticus, Numbers,* and *Deuteronomy*—memorized. At that point, the vast majority of students went home. They would apprentice in the family business or help run the farm.

But the best and brightest would go on to a second level of education, called *bet midrash* ("the house of learning"), where they would continue their studies. By the age of seventeen, they would have memorized—wait for it—*the entire Old Testament.*[15]

Now, at this point, the overwhelming majority were done and were basically told to "go make babies, pray that they become rabbis, and ply your trade."[16] But the best of the best *of the best* would apply to apprentice under a rabbi. Now, this was *really* hard to get into. Apprenticeship programs were the equivalent of the Ivy League today but even more exclusive. You had to find a rabbi whose yoke you were drawn to and then beg to join his band of students. The rabbi would grill you: "How well do you know the Torah?" "What's your take on the Nephilim in Genesis 6?" "Do you side with Hillel or Shammai on Deuteronomy 24?" "Tell me, how often do you pray?"

And *if* he thought you had the smarts, the work ethic, and the chutzpah to one day become a rabbi yourself, he would say something like "Come, follow me."[17] Or another way to translate that is "Come, apprentice under me."

Now, let's say you were one of the lucky few who became an apprentice to a rabbi. From that day on, your entire life was organized around three driving goals:

1. To be with your rabbi

Jesus himself invited his disciples to "be with him."[18]

You would leave your family, your village, your trade, and follow your rabbi *twenty-four seven*. You were a student, but class wasn't MWF from 11–11:50am. "Class" was *life*. You would spend every waking moment with your rabbi—sleeping at his side, eating at his table, sitting at his feet—and end up, after long hours walking behind him from town to town, covered in his dust.

All. Day. Every. Day.

2. To become like your rabbi

Jesus had this great line about how "the apprentice is not above the rabbi, but everyone who is fully trained will be like their rabbi."[19]

That was the heart and soul of apprenticeship—being with your master *for the purpose of becoming like your master*. You would copy his tone of voice, his mannerisms, his figures of speech. You wanted to be him.

Finally, your goal was . . .

3. To do as your rabbi did

The whole point of apprenticeship was to train under a rabbi in order to one day become a rabbi yourself. If you made it through the gauntlet of discipleship (and that was a real *if*), then, when he thought you were ready, your rabbi would turn to you and say something like "Okay, kid, I give you my blessing. Go, and make disciples."

This was what it meant to be a disciple.

This is *still* what it means to be a disciple.

The problem is, this is *not* what most Christians mean by *discipleship* today. (Keep reading.) Yet when you look at Jesus' model, whether in first-century Israel or twenty-first-century America, or wherever you're reading this, the meaning of *discipleship* is perfectly clear: To follow Jesus is to become his apprentice. It's to organize your entire life around three driving goals:

1. Be with Jesus.

2. Become like him.

3. Do as he did.

Apprenticeship to Jesus—that is, following Jesus—is a *whole*-life process of being with Jesus for the purpose of becoming like him and carrying on his work in the world. It's a lifelong journey in which we gradually learn to say and do the kinds of things Jesus said and did as we apprentice under him in every facet of our lives.

Put another way, *disciple* is a noun.

Disciple is a noun, not a verb

The problem with the word *disciple* is that we don't use it much outside church circles. The Hebrew word is *talmid,* and it simply means "a student of a teacher or philosopher"— not just a learner but a practitioner of an embodied way of life, one who is diligently working to be with and become like their master.[20]

I would argue that the best word for translating *talmid* into English is the one I've been using for the last few pages: *apprentice.* This is *such* a helpful word. It conjures up a mode of education that is intentional, embodied, relational, and practice based—a type of learning that is totally different than what I grew up with.

Jesus' model of apprenticeship was a far cry from our Western educational system. As one pair of scholars put it, "Learning wasn't so much about retaining data as it was about gaining essential wisdom for living, absorbing it from those around him. This was . . . the ancient method whereby rabbis trained their *talmidim,* or disciples."[21] To follow Jesus, then, meant to walk alongside him in a posture of listening, learning, observation, obedience, and imitation.[22] For Jesus' first apprentices, the goal wasn't to pass a test, get a degree, or receive a certificate to frame on your office wall; it was to master the art of living in God's good world by learning from Jesus how to make steady progress into the kingdom of God. It was less like learning chemistry and more like learning jujitsu.

But whatever translation you adopt—disciple, apprentice, practitioner, student, follower—let me state the obvious: *Talmid* is a *noun,* not a verb.[23]

People regularly ask me, "Who are you discipling?" or "Who discipled you?" But as far as I can tell, not one time in the entire New Testament is *disciple* used as a verb. Not once.[24] Grammatically speaking, then, to use *disciple* as a verb is bad form.

Case in point: just attempt to use any of its synonyms as a verb . . .

Christian: "Who are you Christian-ing?"

Wait, what? Christian isn't something you *do;* it's someone you *are.*

Believer: "Who are you believer-ing?"

Help me out here, I don't get it. Do you believe (trust in Jesus) or not?

Follower: "Who are you follower-ing?"

I'm so confused: You either follow Jesus or you don't.

People have come to me actually *bitter* because their former pastors "did not disciple" them. What they usually mean is that these pastors didn't spend one-on-one time with them. While I'm *all for* pastors giving their time to foster people's growth in Jesus, I would argue that you can't "disciple" somebody any more than you can "Christian" them, "believer-er" them, or "follower-er" them.

Please hear me: This is *not* just semantics. Language matters.

Here's why: If *disciple* is something that is done *to* you (a verb),[25] then that puts the onus of responsibility for your spiritual formation on *someone else,* like your pastor, church, or mentor. But if *disciple* is a *noun*—if it's someone you *are* or are not—then no one can "disciple" you but Rabbi Jesus himself.

You must choose to accept Jesus' invitation to a life of apprenticeship.

If you choose to enroll as his student (and I very much hope you do), that means when you wake up tomorrow morning, your *entire* life is architected to this threefold aim: to be with Jesus, to become like him, and to do as he did. This is *the* animating passion of your existence. "The rest are just details," as Einstein said.

Tragically, this is not the same thing as being a Christian.

Are you a Christian or an apprentice?

The word *Christian* is used only three times in the New Testament.

To put that in perspective, the word *disciple* (or *apprentice*) is used 269 times, which comes as no surprise since the New Testament was written *by* apprentices of Jesus, *for* apprentices of Jesus.[26]

Just to make it crystal clear . . .

> Christian: 3x
> Apprentice: 269x

The word *Christian* literally means "little Christ" (or "mini Messiah"), which is beautiful. It was originally used as a religious epithet to mock followers of the Way. But over time, our spiritual ancestors embraced the slur and used it to self-identify as those devoted to the imitation of Christ. Goal #2: become like Jesus. All good.

Here's the problem: That is *no longer* what the word conveys to many people today. To many in the West, a Christian is just someone who mentally ascribes to the bare bones of *Christianity* (a word never used in Scripture) and may or may not occasionally attend church.

In Michael Burkhimer's book *Lincoln's Christianity,* he wrote about the long-running debate over whether President Lincoln was a Christian. (The spiritual writer John Ortberg referenced this and noted how Lincoln has become a kind of Rorschach test that says more about what *we* believe than what he believed.[27] Touché.) Burkhimer said that before you can decide about Lincoln's Christianity, you must first confront "the essential question of what it means to be a Christian." He went on to define a Christian as one who believes that "Jesus Christ was divine and part of a Trinity, that Christ died for the sins of the world, and that faith in this doctrine is necessary for one to gain salvation"; and then said, this "is a foundation almost all are familiar with."[28]

Now, I believe all of the above, as do pretty much all followers of Jesus everywhere. But what's striking about this "foundation" that "almost all are familiar with" is that it includes *absolutely nothing about following Jesus and intending to obey him.*

→ *exactly what I haven't been able to articulate*

Hence the rub.

The thing is, the label *Christian* is one Jesus never used. He said, "Whoever wants to be my *apprentice* . . ." not "Whoever wants to put your hand up to become a Christian . . ."

Now, stay with me; happy thoughts are coming soon. Let's frame this problem as it pertains to my country, the United States of America.[29] Around 63 percent of Americans self-identify as Christians, though this number continues to decline.[30] Trying to measure a person's level of spirituality is tricky, but quite a few surveys put the number of Americans who are following Jesus at around 4 percent.[31] So . . .

> Christians: 63 percent
> Apprentices: 4 percent

My Catholic friends distinguish between Catholics and "practicing Catholics." The former is more of a cultural or ethnic category, akin to being from Italy or Boston, and the latter is a measure of spiritual devotion.

Could it be time for Protestants to lovingly delineate between Christians and "practicing Christians"? As Saint Maximus said in the seventh century, a time not all that different from our own, "A person who is simply a man of faith is [not] a disciple."[32]

If an apprentice is simply anyone whose ultimate aim is to be with Jesus in order to become like him and live the way Jesus would live if he were in their shoes, then a *non*-apprentice (whether they identify as an atheist, a devotee of another religion, or even as a Christian) is simply anyone whose ultimate aim in life is *anything else.*

The problem is, in the West, we have created a cultural milieu *where you can be a Christian but not an apprentice of Jesus.*

Much preaching of the gospel today does not call people to a life of discipleship. Following Jesus is seen as *optional*—a post-conversion "second track" for those who want to go further. Tragically, this has created a two-tier church, where a large swath of people who believe in God and even regularly attend church have not re-architected their daily lives on the foundation of apprenticeship to Jesus.[33]

This is an alien idea in the writings of the New Testament. For example, in the literary design of the Gospels, you have two recurring groups: the apprentices and the crowds.[34] The apprentices included all Jesus' followers—the twelve apostles, but also many others, including women. The crowds were simply everyone *else.* There is no third category of "Christians" who generally agree with most of what Jesus was saying but don't follow him or make a serious attempt to obey his teachings (but it's all good 'cause they will "go to heaven when they die").

This sharp divide between the apprentices and the crowds is a rhetorical device used by all four of Jesus' biographers. The ambiguity of the term *crowds* is intentional. It's a way of saying to the reader, "Which group are you in?"

Are you a face in the crowd?

Or an apprentice of Jesus?

Two millennia later, *especially* in the West, this question is more important than ever. I've been saving this Dallas Willard quote for pages . . .

> The greatest issue facing the world today, with all its heartbreaking needs, is whether those who . . . are identified as "Christians" will become *disciples*—students, apprentices, practitioners—*of Jesus Christ,* steadily learning from him how to live the life of the Kingdom of the Heavens into every corner of human existence.[35]

I could not agree more: *The greatest issue facing the world today* is not climate change, surveillance capitalism, human rights, or the specter of nuclear war, as utterly crucial as all these are. But can you imagine how many of those problems would effectively be solved overnight if the *billions* of living humans who identify as Christians all became apprentices of Jesus? If their driving aim was to approach every challenge as Jesus would?

You see, Jesus is not looking for converts to Christianity; he's looking for apprentices in the kingdom of God.

Is he looking for this 1st?

But what are we saved *to*?

I came of age at a fascinating time in the history of the North American church. Every year, more than a million millennials walk away from the faith. And of the millennials who grew up in evangelical churches (like myself), only 10 percent qualify as what the Barna Group has labeled "resilient disciples"—which, sadly, does not mean they are the next Mother Teresa or Martin Luther King Jr.; it just means they are basic followers of Jesus.[36]

Friends, 10 percent is a serious problem.

But what if this crisis of discipleship is a *feature* of evangelicalism, not a bug? What if it's *exactly what we should expect* based on how many people understand the gospel itself?[37]

Short history tour: From at least World War II on, in many circles, the gospel was preached in such a way that a person could become a Christian without becoming an apprentice of Jesus. As I said, discipleship was optional—something to consider later if one were into that sort of thing. Many "converts" then felt that evangelism was a bait and switch: You come for the "free gift" of eternal life, raise your hand and pray the prayer, but then you are told to "deny yourself, take up your cross, and follow Jesus." The problem is, *that's not what people signed up for.*

This split between evangelism and discipleship is still dominant in a large swath of Western churches.

Why am I saying this? Because how you understand the gospel is the linchpin of how you approach (or don't approach) discipleship. "Saying yes to Jesus" does not an apprentice make.

This raises questions about the nature of salvation itself: What exactly are we saved *to*? To even *ask* this question is tantamount to heresy in many streams of the church, but it must be done. Because if we get the gospel wrong, we get discipleship wrong—or we don't get it at all.

Full disclosure: The following is a caricature designed to sharpen my point,[38] but this is the "gospel" as it is presented in many circles . . .

> You are a sinner going to hell.
>
> God loves you.
>
> Jesus died on the cross for your sins.
>
> If you believe in him, you can go to heaven when you die.[39]

Now, much could be said about this "gospel"—namely, that it doesn't sound anything at all like the gospel Jesus himself preached. (Keep reading . . .) Yet everything in it is "biblical," although in desperate need of nuance. I believe it. The problem is not that it's untrue but that it's *missing* whole pieces of truth that are really, really important. It simply does not come close to the full picture of salvation we find in Jesus' preaching or the writings of the New Testament. And it has created a kind of salvation by "minimum entrance requirements."[40]

As you would imagine, there are serious problems with this view of salvation.

There is no guarantee that you *can* be a Christian but not an apprentice of Jesus and still "go to heaven when you die." Jesus warned us, "Not everyone who says to me, 'Lord, Lord,' will enter the kingdom of heaven, but only the one who does the will of my Father who is in heaven."[41]

Even if you can (and I'm nothing but hopeful when it comes to the mercy of God), you remain trapped in a self-defeating cycle of sin and shame. And you never experience the life with God and formation into a person of love that we all ache for in the marrow of our bones.

Much has been said in the Western church about the forgiveness of sins, which is good. Sin, as we'll explore in the pages to come, is *the* major obstacle on the path to becoming a person of love. But what is sin? We're regularly told that the word *sin* (*hamartia* in Greek) means "to miss the mark."[42] True. But this begs the question, What is *the mark*?

Is it moral perfection? Is it a full ledger before the court of heaven? Is it not breaking any of the commands laid down in the Bible?

What if the mark is union with God?

What if it's the healing of your soul through participation in the inner life of the Trinity?

What if it's adoption into the Father's new multiethnic family through the saving work of his Son, Jesus?

What if it's becoming the kind of person who is so pervaded by love, wisdom, and strength that we have developed the capacity to eventually rule with Jesus over the cosmos itself?

If so, this gospel is an inadequate foundation on which to build a life of apprenticeship that is conducive to deep inner healing and overall transformation of body and soul.

And there it is—the fatal flaw: This version of the gospel *has* no call to apprentice yourself to Jesus. It normally requires you to say a one-time prayer, believe a set of doctrines about God, and attend church, thereby ensuring you go to heaven when you die. But in a bizarre twist, it does not necessarily require a life of apprenticeship to Jesus in the here and now.

When Jesus said he "came to seek and to save the lost,"[43] is this the salvation he had in mind? A cursory reading of the Gospels would indicate we're wildly underestimating all that Jesus intends for us . . .

For Jesus, salvation is less about getting *you into heaven* and more about getting *heaven into you*.

It's not just about *him* becoming like *us* but also about *us* becoming like *him*.

It's less of a *transaction* and more of a *transformation*.

It's not just about what he has done *for* us but also about what he has done, is doing, and will do *in* us if we apprentice under him.

It's about being a person who not only is loved *by* God but also is pervaded by the love *of* God.

It's not just accepting the merit of his *death* but also receiving the power of his *resurrection*.

And it's not just about you and me as *individuals* but also about the formation of a whole new humanity and the healing of *the cosmos itself.*

But, again, the main problem with this "gospel" is that it simply *does not sound anything like the gospel Jesus preached.*

Listen to Mark's summary of Jesus' gospel:

> "The time has come," he said. "The kingdom of God has come near. Repent and believe the good news!"[44]

Jesus' gospel was that Israel's long story had reached its climax in him—that he had come to reunite heaven and earth and usher in the kingdom of God, a God-saturated society of peace and justice and love. Jesus' central message was that this in-breaking kingdom is available *now,* to all. That *anyone,* no matter who you are, where you come from, or what your station in life is, can enter this kingdom and be "blessed" (or "happy") with God. You can have this new kind of life if you will put your trust and confidence in Jesus for the whole of your life.

Is this how you understand the gospel?

In Jesus' gospel, the call to become an apprentice makes perfect sense. If the kingdom of God is "near" but is not a kingdom with borders and passports—in fact, it's been "hidden . . . from the wise and learned"[45]—then it makes sense that we'd need some serious training in *how* to access this extraordinary new society and enter the inner life of God that's been made available to us through Jesus. We'd need access to a new power to break off our old life habits (that belong to the kingdom of this world) and become who we were always meant to be: people of the new kingdom. We'd want to learn from the absolute best—Jesus himself. In short, we'd want to become his apprentices.

One way to judge the veracity of your gospel is by this simple acid test: Would someone hearing your gospel naturally conclude that apprenticeship to Jesus is the only fitting response?

Much has been said about the rise of consumer Christianity in recent decades, but much *less* has been said about its possible connection to the way the gospel has been preached. The relationship of some Western Christians to the gospel is passive. We are often told, "It's not about what you do; it's about what Jesus *has done for you.*" But that's a false dichotomy, and that language is never used by *any* of the New Testament writers. It seems the Western church has at times been more careful to avoid "works righteousness" than to avoid sin.

Don't get me wrong; the Gospels are full of story after story of *compassion.* In Jesus' parables, we're the servant whose debt of billions is forgiven by the king, the prodigal who is welcomed home with a feast after we've squandered our father's inheritance, and the beggar outside the gate who is seated at Abraham's table as the guest of honor. It's always been grace, pure grace.

But Jesus didn't go around beating up on self-effort. As the saying goes, "Grace is not opposed to *effort,* it is opposed to *earning.*"[46] Don't conflate the two.

Jesus ended the Sermon on the Mount with this famous climax:

> Everyone who hears these words of mine and does not
> put them into practice [note his word choice: *practice*] is
> like a foolish man who built his house on sand. The rain
> came down, the streams rose, and the winds blew and
> beat against that house, and it fell with a great crash.[47]

Can you imagine Jesus, to stave off any soteriological anxiety, immediately adding, "But don't worry. I'm about to do it all for you. You don't need to do a thing, because that would be works-based righteousness and it's bad"?

It's unimaginable that Jesus would ever say something like that.

Sadly, this tragic misunderstanding of salvation "tends to produce consumers of Jesus' merit" rather than "disciples of Jesus' Way."[48]

On that note . . .

A way of life

The original name for the community of Jesus' apprentices was "the Way" or "followers of the Way."

> Acts 9v2: "[Saul] asked him for letters to the syna-
> gogues in Damascus, so that if he found any there who
> belonged to the Way . . ."

Acts 19v23: "About that time there arose a great disturbance about the Way."

Acts 24v14: "I worship the God of our ancestors as a follower of the Way."

These are just a few examples. The Greek word for "way" is *hodos*. The word literally means "a road or path," but Jesus used it as a metaphor for apprenticeship to him.

In this word picture is a simple but revolutionary idea: The Way of Jesus is not just a theology (a set of ideas that we believe in our heads). It *is* that, but it's more.

And it's not just ethics (a list of dos and don'ts that we obey or disobey). It *is* that, but it's still more.

It's exactly what it sounds like—*a way of life*.

One way to paraphrase Jesus' invitation to "follow me" is to say, "Adopt my overall way of life to experience the *life* I have on offer."

I love this from the Eastern Orthodox bishop Kallistos Ware:

> Christianity is more than a theory about the universe, more than teachings written down on paper; it is a path along which we journey—in the deepest and richest sense, the *way of life*.[49]

So often in the church, much is said about what to believe and what is right or wrong (which I'm all for), but *so little* is said about a lifestyle that is conducive to life with God. Yet *lifestyle* is where the money is.

Jesus famously said,

> I am the way and the truth and the life.[50]

People misread this as a statement about who's in or out and who's going to hell and who's en route to heaven, but that's not likely what Jesus meant. It's far more likely he was saying that the marriage of his truth (his teaching) and his way (his lifestyle) is how to get to the with-God *life* he offers.

As the Presbyterian pastor Eugene Peterson once said, "The Jesus way wedded to the Jesus truth brings about the Jesus life." He then concluded, "Jesus as the truth gets far more attention than Jesus as the way. Jesus as the way is the most frequently evaded metaphor among the Christians with whom I have worked for fifty years as a North American pastor."[51]

There is a way of life—modeled personally by Jesus himself—that is *far* beyond anything else on offer in this world. It can open you up to God's presence and power in ways most people only dream. But it requires you to follow a path marked out for you by Jesus himself. Jesus also said,

> Enter through the narrow gate. For wide is the gate and broad is the road [*hodos* / way] that leads to destruction, and many enter through it. But small is the gate and narrow the road [*hodos* / way] that leads to life, and only a few find it.[52]

One interpretation of this teaching is that only a few people are "going to heaven when they die" and that everyone else is on the train to the eternal torture chamber. Here's a different interpretation that I find more compelling: The Way of Jesus is "narrow," meaning, it is *a very specific way to live*. And if you follow it, it will lead you to *life,* both in this age and the age to come.

The "broad" way is that of the majority culture, which is as simple as it is crass: "Follow the crowd and do whatever you want." Billions of people live this way, but it does *not* lead them to life; instead, it often leads to destruction. It leads to countless stories of people falling to pieces and never reaching their promise or potential—what Jesus called "eternal life," which describes not just *quantity* but *quality* of life. This eternal life is a new way to be human through union with God, beginning now and stretching over the horizon of death into forever.

Jesus was constantly offering this life to any who would follow him. "I have come that they may have life, and have it *to the full*,"[53] he said. So much life that our "cup overflows."[54]

It seems that it's almost always a minority who say yes to Jesus' invitation. But you can be one of the lucky few—an apprentice of Jesus.

Because this staggering offer of life is available to *all*.

Whoever means *whoever*

Jesus would regularly stand in front of large crowds and make this invitation:

> Whoever wants to be my disciple must deny them-selves and take up their cross and follow me.[55]

Notice the opening word: *whoever*. That would have been electrifying to Jesus' hearers. Remember what I said earlier about how only the best of the best *of the best* got to apprentice under a rabbi? Like an elite university today, rabbis were highly selective about whom they accepted as students because the quality of the students reflected on the quality of the teacher. As a rule, a rabbi would *never* risk rejection; he would do the rejecting.

Not Rabbi Jesus.

Whoever.

And whoever meant *whoever*—fisherman, Zealot, tax collector, even betrayer. Torah devotee or sex worker. Religious bigot or woman caught in the act of adultery. Intellectual elite or blind beggar on the side of the road. Jesus invited *all* to apprentice under him into life in the kingdom of God.

And nothing's changed over time: We're all *still* invited, no matter who we are or what we've done. Oppressed or oppressor. Upwardly mobile or entrenched in poverty. Polymath or high school dropout. Fastidious health nut or addict. Mentally sound or not. Virgin or sexually promiscuous. Married, divorced, or divorced again. Hyper-religious or fallen away. Full of faith or racked by doubt.

Whoever means *whoever*.

Now we're finally ready to circle back to the question we began part 1 with: What would prompt Simon to drop his net on the beach, walk away from his career, and follow Jesus all on a moment's notice?

Are you kidding me? he would have thought. *This is the chance of a lifetime.*

Let me attempt a clumsy adaptation from our era: Imagine you're a high school dropout who always dreamed of becoming a professor. You wanted desperately to go to college, but you couldn't get accepted. Now imagine you're working a dead-end job in food service: low hourly wage and long, monotonous days. One day as you're watching the clock from behind the cash register, a world-famous professor from a prestigious university walks through the door on a pit stop from his worldwide book tour. He takes an instant liking to you and says, "If you come with me right now, you can become my student. I'll give you a full-ride scholarship. You can live in my home and study under me. And I'll teach you everything I know and give you access to all my resources. I believe that you have the capacity to one day do what I do. It will be the hardest thing you've ever done, but it will pay dividends you cannot possibly imagine. But you have to come with me now."

What would you do? What anyone in their right mind would do: Throw your apron on the floor, dance a Scottish jig, and *run* out the door behind him.

Simon and Andrew were fishermen. Think about that for a second: This means they *didn't* make it into an apprenticeship program. They *weren't* the best of the best of the best; they were the ones who got sent home to "make babies and pray they become rabbis."

But Jesus invited them to become his apprentices.

Before they believed in Jesus, he believed in *them*.

I've never attempted Alexandre Dumas's sixteen-hundred-page tome *The Count of Monte Cristo,*[56] but the movie with Jim Caviezel is one of my favorites. Caviezel's character, Edmond Dantès, is betrayed by his best friend and unjustly incarcerated in the island prison Château d'If. He falls into an unlikely friendship with Abbé Faria, a fellow inmate and priest. Dantès is drawn to the priest but turned off by his faith in Jesus. My favorite scene in the movie is when, with his dying breath, Abbé Faria tells Dantès not to use the treasure for revenge, for "God said, 'Vengeance is mine.'"

"I don't believe in God," replies Dantès.

Then comes the priest's haunting line: "It doesn't matter. He believes in you."[57]

We talk a lot about the call to believe in Jesus—to put your trust and confidence in him to lead you to life. This is good and fitting. But it must also be said that *Jesus believes in you.* He believes that you can become his apprentice. Starting right where you are, you can follow him into a life in the kingdom that fulfills your deepest desires.

He believes that you can live under the loving gaze of the Father; you can also become the kind of person who is *like* the Father— loving and joyful and full of peace, patience, and kindness. You can grow into a person of happiness, even in times of great suffering. The kind of person who is not afraid of suffering or even of death, who is free of the emotional need for things to go your own way. You can fulfill your purpose. You can even learn to do many of the incredible things Jesus did. To see the signs of his kingdom manifest in your ordinary life.

It's possible—all of it.

But it's not *inevitable*.

It won't just happen by chance.

There are no accidental saints.

You can't just slip your hand up at the end of a sermon. It's a high bar of entry: It will require you to reorder your entire life around following Jesus as your undisputed top priority, over your job, your money, your reputation—over everything. Yet all these things will find their rightful place once integrated into a life of apprenticeship.

This life can be *your* life.

All you have to do is let go of your nets . . .

Practicing the Way—

Goal #1: Be with Jesus

—

Years ago, a Jesuit priest named Father Rick was kind enough to offer me spiritual direction. He was old and wise and full of insight, but the thing I most remember about our times together is how peaceful he was. When I was with him, I would literally feel my heart rate slow down, my body calm, and my anxiety dissipate. It's like he set the atmosphere in the room, and just breathing the same air cleaned out my soul.

Just being *with* him did something *to* me.

It comes as no surprise that Jesus began the formation of his apprentices by simply calling them to "come, follow me"—to just walk alongside him on the Way.

In John 1, he invited Andrew and his friend to merely come and see where he was staying. "So they came and saw where he was staying, and they stayed with him that day."[1]

In Luke 10v39, we read of an apprentice named Mary "who sat at the Lord's feet listening to what he said."[2]

In Mark 3, Jesus "called" his disciples, and "they came to him." This would have been a group of dozens or even hundreds of followers who spent long swaths of time with Jesus. From this larger pool of disciples, Jesus chose twelve for special training so that "they might *be with him*."[3]

This is the first and most important goal of apprenticeship to Jesus: to be *with* him, to spend every waking moment aware of his presence and attentive to his voice. To cultivate a with-ness to Jesus as the baseline of your entire life.

Following Jesus is *not* a three-step formula: be with him, become like him, and so on. *But* there is a sequence. It is not a program but a progression. First, you come and be with Jesus; gradually you start to become *like* him; eventually, it's like you can't help it—you begin to do the kinds of things he did in the world. We see this progression in the stories of the original disciples: They spent months or possibly years just following him around Israel and sitting at his feet. *Very* slowly they began to change, and eventually, he "sent them out" to preach.[4]

Maybe you're new to following Jesus and you're thinking, *Where do I even start?* You start *here,* with goal #1: Be with Jesus.

But how exactly does this work *now*? I mean, "Follow me" wasn't a metaphor when it originally came from Jesus' lips. It was literal, as in "I'm walking east along the Wadi Qelt to Jericho. Walk behind me." But we can't book a flight to Tel Aviv, rent a car, go find Jesus on a mountainside, and sit down at his feet.

So, how do we be *with* him?

"Abide in me"

The night before his death, Jesus made a puzzling promise to his apprentices:

I will ask the Father, and he will give you another advocate to help you and *be with you* forever.[5]

Short exegesis: The phrase "another advocate" is hard to translate
into English. The Greek word for "another" is *allos,* and it literally means "another of the same kind"[6] or "another one of me."
The word for "advocate" is *paraklētos,* and it can be translated
"helper" or "intercessor."[7]

So, the Father will give us another one of Jesus? To be with us?
To help us and intercede for us?

Exactly.

A few sentences later, Jesus named this mysterious "another
one of me" as "the Holy Spirit."[8] Translation: Going forward,
the way Jesus' apprentices are to "be with him" is via the
Holy Spirit.

Now, short theology sidebar: In the library of Scripture, the Holy
Spirit is not a vague force like in Star Wars, an eternal sea of
nonbeing as in Eastern mysticism, or a nice feeling one gets in
prayer. In Jesus' teachings, the Spirit is a he, not an it. That
doesn't mean the Spirit is male; it means that the Spirit is a
person.

In all of Jesus' teachings, what we call God is, in a mysterious but
beautiful way, a flow of love between the Father and the Son and
the Holy Spirit. God is a community of self-giving love; each
member of the Trinity, as theologians call them, is distinct yet
somehow still one. To be with the Spirit *is* to be with Jesus, and
to be with Jesus is to be with the Father. It's to enter the flow of
love within the inner life of God himself.

Let's return to the story: Goal #1 of apprenticeship to Jesus is to live in that moment-by-moment flow of love within the Trinity. Again, if there's a starting line, this is it.

But Jesus gave his apprentices more than a promise; he gave them a practice.

Just a few moments later, Jesus gave a teaching that is essentially a tutorial on how to be with him. You could title it "Jesus' Model of Spiritual Formation." He used the metaphor of a winery and the need for a branch to "abide" in the vine to "bear much fruit." In this metaphor, Jesus is the vine, and we his apprentices are the branches.

Then he gave this instruction:

Abide in me, and I in you.[9]

The word for "abide" is *menō* in Greek; it can be translated "remain" or "stay" or "dwell" or "make your home in."[10] We could translate the verse like this: "Make your home in me, as I make my home in you."

Jesus uses this word *menō* not once but *ten times* in this short teaching. Go read it. He's driving to a singular point: Make your home in my presence by the Spirit, and never leave.

Now, if this sounds like the purview of monks and nuns, not the rest of us who are busy raising kids or living in a city or responsible for an inbox, let me clarify: *Jesus isn't asking you to do something you're not already doing.*

All of us are abiding.

The question isn't, Are you abiding?

It's, What are you abiding *in*?

All of us have a source we are rooted in, a kind of default setting we return to. An emotional home. It's where our minds go when they're not busy with tasks, where our feelings go when we need solace, where our bodies go when we have free time, and where our money goes after we pay the bills.

We will make our home somewhere, the question is "Where?"

And this matters, because whatever we "abide" in will determine the "fruit" of our lives, for good or for ill.

If we are rooted in the infinite scroll of social media, it will *form* us, likely into people who are angry, anxious, arrogant, simplistic, and distracted.[11]

If we are rooted in the endless queues of our streaming platforms of choice, they will form us too, likely into people who are lustful, restless, and bored, never present to what *is* . . .

If we are rooted in the pursuit of hedonism—another drink, another toke, or another hookup to take the edge off the pain and let us find a moment's peace—that will form us as well, likely into people who are compulsive, addictive, and running from our pain and, simultaneously, our healing.

Insert examples ad nauseam.

But if we are rooted in the inner life of God . . . that will also form us. It will slowly grow the "fruit of the Spirit" in our life:

"love, joy, peace, forbearance, kindness, goodness, faithfulness, gentleness and self-control."[12]

Where is your emotional home?

What do you return to in your quiet moments? Where do you go to find solace and joy? What would it look like for you to make your home inside God?

And to clarify, this is not about holing up in a monastery but about learning to always be in two places at once . . .

Eating your breakfast and being with Jesus . . .

Braving public transit for your morning commute and being with Jesus . . .

Changing *another* diaper and being with Jesus . . .

Sorting through your inbox yet still being with Jesus . . .

Cooking dinner for your family or friends and resting your heart in Jesus . . .

Apprenticeship to Jesus is about turning your body into a temple, a place of overlap between heaven and earth—an advance sign of what one day Jesus will do for the entire cosmos, when heaven and earth are at long last reunited as one. This is the single most extraordinary opportunity in the entire universe: to let your body become God's home. And it's set before you every single day.

Jesus called this way of life "abiding," but the saints and sages have used all sorts of language down through history to capture the extraordinary possibility of this invitation.

Paul called it prayer "without ceasing."[13]

The Spanish Carmelite Saint John of the Cross called it "silent love" and urged us to "remain in loving attention on God."

Madame Guyon—the French mystic—called it a "continuous inner act of abiding."

The old Quakers called it "centering down,"[14] as if abiding was getting in touch with the bedrock of all reality.

The Jesuit spiritual director Jean-Pierre de Caussade called it "the sacrament of the present moment," as if each moment with God is its own Eucharist, its own movable feast.[15]

A. W. Tozer called it "habitual, conscious communion" and said, "At the heart of the Christian message is God Himself waiting for His redeemed children to push in to conscious awareness of His presence."[16]

Dallas Willard loved to call it "the with-God life."[17]

So many saints, with so many names for life with Jesus.

But my undisputed favorite is from a monk named Brother Lawrence, who called this "the practice of the presence of God."[18]

I love Brother Lawrence's nomenclature. Laced into it is a profound but honest truth: As nice as the *idea* of being with Jesus sounds, it will remain nothing more than a shallow spiritual sentimentality until we accept that abiding is *not a technique* by which we control our relationship with God; but it is *a skill*.

And like all skills, it will take *practice* to master . . .

Turning God into a habit

When you first come awake at the beginning of the day, where does your mind naturally go?

When you lay your head on your pillow after a long, tiring day, what are your final thoughts as you drift off to sleep?

In the little moments of space throughout your day—waiting in line for your morning coffee, stuck in traffic, sitting down to a meal—where does your mind fall "without thinking" about it?

Let's be honest: For most of us, it's not to Jesus.

It's to our wants and needs, our fears, our wounds—to negative rumination. "The undirected mind tends toward chaos." The psychologist Mihaly Csikszentmihalyi called this phenomenon "psychic entropy."[19]

But on this, ancient Christian spirituality and bleeding-edge neuroscience agree: The mind can be *retrained*. Re-formed. Whether you call this process neuroplasticity or "the practice of the presence of God," the powerful truth still stands: Our minds do not *have* to live in a negative spiral; they can be retrained to "abide"—to live in the presence of God.

The monk who coined the phrase "the practice of the presence of God" wasn't a priest; he was a dishwasher in a monastery in seventeenth-century Paris. Brother Lawrence made it his life's ambition to experience God in the chaos of the kitchen, with all its noise, distraction, and busyness. By the end of his life, he said,

The time of busyness does not with me differ from the time of prayer; and in the noise and clatter of my kitchen, while several persons are at the same time calling for different things, I possess God in as great tranquility as if I were upon my knees before the Blessed Sacrament.[20]

Take note: He was a Catholic. The "Blessed Sacrament" (what Protestants call "the Lord's Supper") was *the holiest moment* in the spiritual life. But Brother Lawrence had come to a place where *all* of his life was holy; there was no longer any difference between the quiet of morning prayer and the cacophony of dinner prep, between the sanctity of the altar and the mundanity of the evening meal. Life was a seamless, integrated whole, grounded in God's presence.

We read similar language from the Quaker writer Thomas Kelly:

How, then, shall we . . . live the life of prayer without ceasing? By quiet, persistent practice in turning of all our being, day and night, in prayer and inward worship and surrender, toward Him who calls in the deeps of our souls. Mental habits of inward orientation must be established.[21]

There it is again: by "persistent practice" and "mental habits." Through practice we can train (or retrain) our minds to rest in God amid the entropy of life. But not without the use of habit.

If this life of being with Jesus required practice as far back as the 1600s—four centuries before the iPhone—*how much more so now,* in the age of urban noise pollution and the digital distraction of nonstop alerts, notifications, and an "ecosystem of interruption technologies."[22] *This will not just happen.* But listen, it *can* happen, *if* you practice.

Let me offer you this from Dallas Willard . . .

> The first and most basic thing we can and must do is to keep God before our minds. . . . This is *the* fundamental secret of caring for our souls. Our part in thus practicing the presence of God is to direct and redirect our minds constantly to Him. In the early time of our practicing, we may well be challenged by our burdensome habits of dwelling on things less than God [that is, will be constantly distracted by a million other things]. But these are habits—not the law of gravity— and can be broken. A new, grace-filled habit will replace the former ones as we take intentional steps toward keeping God before us. Soon our minds will return to God as the needle of a compass constantly returns to the north. . . . If God is the great longing of our souls, He will become the polestar of our inward beings.[23]

He's talking about turning God into a habit.

I love Willard's word picture of a compass that "constantly returns to the north." We can habituate our minds, which scientists define as our directed attention (what we give our focus to), to constantly return to God . . .

What Willard and all these spiritual masters of the Way are saying is that through *habit* you can co-create with Jesus a mind that is fixed on God all through the day. You can say with the psalmist, "I have set the LORD always before me."[24] Or with Paul, "Set your minds on things above."[25]

Each time you get a little mental breath in the busyness of your life—that split second after you hit send on the email, the moment when you come to a red light, or those first conscious thoughts when you awake from sleep—through deliberate practice, you can train your mind to come back to God, come back to God, *come back to God* . . .

Eventually your mind—and through it, your entire body and soul—will anchor itself in God, will "abide." Even in all the noise and chaos of the modern world, with its traffic to suffer, meetings to attend, and babies to feed, you can develop a mind that is rooted in God.

If the mind is a kind of portal to the soul and if "you become what you contemplate," as Hwee Hwee Tan so beautifully put it,[26] then few things could be more important. Indeed, our destiny could hang in the balance.

Now, I recognize that turning God into a habit may sound about as inspiring as turning romance or laughter or poetry into a habit. In a culture that equates authenticity with spontaneous emotions,[27] habit is a tough sell. But show me a person's habits, and I will show you what they are *truly* most passionate about, most dedicated to, most willing to suffer for, and most in love with.

And I will show you who they will become.

Again, when you have that fleeting mental break, that blessed white space of thought, where does your mind go? Does it go to God? To the Father's love pouring out toward you in Christ and by the Spirit, deep within and all around you?

If not, it can: The human mind is *far more moldable* than most of us were led to believe. It can be changed to a new default setting, a new baseline. To a new God-orientation.

Before the neuroscientist Dr. Donald Hebb famously said, "Neurons that fire together wire together" (what neuroscientists now call "Hebb's rule"), A. W. Tozer said that as we "set the direction of our hearts toward Jesus," something miraculous takes place in our inner beings: "A habit of soul is forming which will become, after a while, a sort of spiritual reflex requiring no more conscious effort on our part."[28] Or as the missionary Frank Laubach testified, "This simple practice requires only a gentle pressure of the will, not more than a person can exert easily. *It grows easier as the habit becomes fixed.*"[29]

I'm no spiritual master, but after practicing this for over a decade, I can confirm their hypothesis from personal experience: It really does grow easier.

I begin each morning in prayer and have a daily prayer rhythm I live by, but like most people, I spend large parts of my day getting sucked into hurry and distraction. Yet when I slow down, when my mind comes to rest, more and more I find my consciousness naturally going "home" to God.

Should you pursue this, the early days of "practicing the presence of God" will likely be difficult and humbling, yet joyful—difficult because we *all* forget God constantly and get sucked back into hurry; humbling for the same reason, but full of joy and happiness as we begin to tap into the deepest ache of our souls: the desire for God. Over time, the wiring of your brain will begin to change, to heal from its rupture from your maker. New neural pathways will form. The more you pray, the more you *think* to pray. What first felt almost impossible eventually will become as easy and natural as breathing.

There is so much we *can't* do in our spiritual formation; we cannot fix or heal or transform ourselves. But we *can* do this: We can be with Jesus. We can pause for little moments throughout our days and turn our hearts toward Jesus in silent prayer and love.

You can do this—*if you are willing to practice*. As apprentices of Jesus, you and I have both the *ability* and the *responsibility* to set our minds on him. To direct the inner gaze of our hearts onto his love.

To look at him, looking at us, in love . . .

"I look at Him, He looks at me, and we are happy"

The retreat leader and spiritual director Marjorie Thompson tells the story of a conversation between an eighteenth-century priest and an elderly peasant who would sit alone for long hours in the quiet of the church. When the priest asked what he was doing, the old man simply replied, "I look at Him, He looks at me, and we are happy."[30]

This is the apex of Christian spirituality. Saint Ignatius of Loyola once called God "Love loving."[31] In doing so, he spoke for the millions of contemplatives down through history who have found sitting in the quiet and letting God love them to be the single most joyful experience this side of eternity; indeed, it is a kind of foretaste *of* eternity.

The fourteenth-century Eastern Orthodox writer Kallistos Katafygiotis said it boldly:

> The most important thing that happens between God and the human soul is to love and to be loved.[32]

Do you believe that?

That *the* most important thing in all of life is to love and be loved by God?

We can be deceived into thinking of abiding as no more than mental hygiene for the prefrontal cortex—the Christianized version of "think happy thoughts." And while the curation of our consciousness toward the good, beautiful, and true is vital to our formation, abiding is not just about our thought lives or even our emotional lives. It's about a level of with-ness to Jesus that goes *beyond* our thoughts and feelings. It's about *love.*

Masters of the Way of Jesus have long called this "contemplation." The word *contemplation* means different things to different people at different times in church history, but at its most basic, it just means looking at God, looking at you, in love.

The word *contemplation* comes straight out of the New Testament itself, from a key passage in Paul's second letter to the Corinthians:

> We all, who with unveiled faces *contemplate* the Lord's glory, are being transformed into his image with ever-increasing glory.[33]

The Greek word for "contemplate" here is *katoptrizō,* and it means to "gaze or behold." To "contemplate the Lord's glory" is to direct the inner gaze of your heart at the Trinitarian community of love. As the psalmist David put it, it's "to gaze on the beauty of the LORD."[34] To the degree we do so, we are "transformed into his image." Meaning, we become like what we gaze at—Jesus. "With ever-increasing glory," meaning, we become more and more beautiful, like Jesus, over time, through simple, daily contemplation.

We'll get to goal #2, "become like Jesus," soon, but let me give you a sneak peek: The question for goal #1, "be with Jesus," was, *How* do we be with Jesus? And the answer was, basically, we abide in the vine; we live rooted in a relational connection to Jesus by the Spirit.

The question for goal #2 is not all that different: *How* do we become like Jesus? A full answer would take a book,[35] but here's the SparkNotes version: through contemplation. We let God love us into people of love.

As a general rule, we become more loving by *experiencing* love, not by hearing about it in a lecture or reading about it in a book. Psychologists' basic rule of thumb is that we are loving to the degree that we have been loved. This is why it's so much easier for those who were well loved by their parents or caregivers in their early years to give and receive love as adults. That said, *no* family of origin is healthy enough to transform us into the kind of love we see in Jesus, *and no family is dysfunctional enough to keep us from* becoming *people of love* in Jesus. *All* of us have the potential to grow and mature into people of *agape.* But to do so, we have to *experience* the love of God.

I think of Paul's prayer for the Ephesians:

I pray that out of his glorious riches he may strengthen you with power through his Spirit in your inner being, so that Christ may dwell in your hearts through faith. And I pray that you, being rooted and established in love, may have power, together with all the Lord's holy people, to grasp how wide and long and high and deep is the love of Christ, and to know this love that surpasses knowledge—that you may be filled to the measure of all the fullness of God.[36]

What a line: "to know this love that surpasses knowledge." Paul wasn't anti-intellectual, not by a long shot. But he was also aware of the limitations of the mind: We can't just know *about* the love of God; we have to *know* the love of God,[37] to experience it in our inner beings, if we are to be transformed into people *of* love.

And in Paul's paradigm, this transformation happens as we "contemplate," as we gaze, as we look at God, looking at us, in love.

This simple, uncomplicated act has the potential to transform our inner lives and heal our deepest wounds in ways that more Bible study, church attendance, and even therapy (as good as those are) cannot possibly touch.

David Benner, a psychologist and spiritual director, said this of his own experience of contemplation:

> Meditating on God's love has done more to increase my love than decades of effort to try to be more loving. Allowing myself to deeply experience his love—taking time to soak in it and allow it to infuse me—has begun to effect changes that I had given up hope of ever experiencing. Coming back to God in my failures at love, throwing myself into his arms and asking him

to remind me of how much he loves me as I am——here I begin to experience new levels of love to give to others.[38]

I will never forget when my spiritual director advised me, "John Mark, sit in your sin and let God love you." He did *not* mean "Keep sinning and don't feel guilty." He meant "*When* you sin [and I will, as you will], don't hide it from God. Hold it before God, with no excuses, no blame shifting, no denial, just utter vulnerability, and let God love you as you *are*. And then let God love you into who you have the potential to *become*."

But this is a very different kind of prayer than many of us are used to. I grew up praying in a mode that was wordy, fast-paced, and a bit demanding. Prayer, to me, meant asking God for things, mostly good things, but still, the aim was to use a lot of words to ask God for what you needed and desired. And there's a place for that.

Yet contemplative prayer isn't looking to get anything *from* God; it's just looking *at* God. "I look at Him, He looks at me, and we are happy."

Few of us even realize this type of prayer is a possibility.

It's this deeper layer of prayer that I find both most challenging and most rewarding. Challenging not because it's unpleasant (the opposite, in fact) but because it requires the very capacity of which our world schemes to rob me: *attention*.

The capacity to set the heart's attention on God—so basic to following Jesus—is the very commodity we are losing to the "attention economy,"[39] trading looking for liking and gazing for doomscrolling. But if we can't pay attention, we can't pray.

The French philosopher Simone Weil defined prayer as "absolutely unmixed attention."[40] The Quaker Douglas Steere said to pray is "to pay attention to the deepest thing [I] know."[41] And Dr. Rich Plass wrote, "Contemplative prayer is a willingness to enjoy and be present to God. *It is a matter of being consciously aware of my presence in Christ and attentive to Christ's presence within me.* It is saying yes to God with my whole being but without words."[42]

It's not that words in prayer are bad; they aren't. It's just that you reach a point in *any* relationship, but especially with God, where words and even thoughts no longer carry you forward toward intimacy. They bring you so far but not all the way. They may even hold you back.

God is not a concept or an emotion, and he's certainly not a doctrine in a statement of faith or a chapter in a theology book; he is a *person,* whose burning desire is to know and be known by you. And like in any intimate relationship, there is a kind of knowledge that goes beyond words—a kind you can get *only* by direct person-to-person experience.[43]

This is where contemplative prayer veers in an entirely different direction from mindfulness and other more popular types of meditation. For example, in Buddhist meditation, the goal is to empty the self; prayer involves a similar emptying, but its goal is to *make room* for a *filling* of God. In mindfulness, the goal is simply to be present in the moment; in prayer, it's to be present *to God's presence* in the moment, and, ultimately, present to his *love.*

This may sound *way* too mystical for your persuasion, but to put all my cards on the table, I'm with the theologian Karl Rahner, who said, "The Christian of the future will be a mystic or he will not exist at all."[44]

You know why I think he's right? Because the Christian of the *past* was a mystic. And if we don't recapture contemplation, we "will not exist at all" in the corrosive soil of the secular West.

I'm aware that the label *mystic* is a turnoff for some people. (People occasionally ask me, "You're not a *mystic,* are you?" I usually slip them a mischievous smile . . .) But I don't mean it in *any* kind of heterodox sense. All I mean by *mystic* is a disciple of Jesus who wants to experience spiritually what is true of them theologically. Scripture is clear: All those who have been baptized are "in Christ."[45] You have been baptized, immersed in the Trinitarian community of Father and Son and Holy Spirit, saturated in God. "Your life is now hidden with Christ in God."[46] Christ is "in you, the hope of glory."[47]

Mystics are just those who aren't content to read books or hear sermons about this glorious reality; they want to *experience* this love and be *transformed* by it into people *of* love. Because it's here—looking at God, God looking at us, in love—that "we are happy," that we are most free, content, at rest, at ease, grateful, joy filled, and alive.

So many Christians simply have no idea of the staggering immensity of God's love for them and of that love's power to transform them into people of love, as well as bring them great happiness and lasting peace. If they knew, they would undoubtedly do *whatever it takes* to make time to be with him.

Unfortunately, many of us still view following Jesus as a means to an end—a ticket to heaven, to nice feelings, to a successful, upwardly mobile life, and so on.

We still don't get it: *He's* the end.

The reward for following Jesus is *Jesus*

Every morning I get up early and begin my day with the ancient Christian spiritual discipline of really good coffee.[48] I go to a little room in my house, close the door, sit cross-legged on the floor, and pray. I usually pray the psalms (note: not *read* the psalms), meditate on a passage of Scripture, talk to God about my life, listen for his voice, and attempt to just let go. But most of the time, I just sit there. I breathe. And I look at what my eyes can't see.

Some days my mind is sharp and alert, my heart is burning for God, and I *feel* God's nearness. Other days (more often than not) my mind is like a "banana tree filled with monkeys," as Henri Nouwen once said[49]—it's all over the place, my heart is troubled and afraid, and I struggle to pay attention.

But *even then,* my time in the quiet is usually the *best* part of my day. Truly. Something dazzling has to happen to outshine it. Because it's here, where I am most deeply aware of God, that I am most happy and at ease.

In our fast-paced, productivity-obsessed, digitally distracted culture that is endlessly chasing the life script of up and to the right, time is money and money is god. So, the idea of slowing down, coming to quiet, dealing with the myriad of distractions within and without, and just letting God love you into a person of love, sounds like a waste of time. In fact, professor James Houston once called prayer "wasting time on God." He didn't mean prayer is a waste; he meant, in a culture like ours, prayer can *feel like* a waste of time. But to those who have discovered the possibility of life with God, it is the pinnacle of human existence. Once you've tasted of prayer—*true* prayer— you realize that deepening your surrender to and honing your attention on God are literally the most important things in the world.

Prayer (that is, being with Jesus) is our primary portal to joy. It's the best part not just of each day but of *life*.

Prayer—of any kind—will always remain a chore, another task on our religious to-do list, until we come to realize that Jesus himself is our "exceedingly great reward."[50] That the reward for following Jesus is, well, Jesus. It's the sheer joy of friendship with him.

Jesus himself said to his disciples, "No longer do I call you servants. . . . I have called you friends."[51] Prayer is how we cultivate this friendship. In his devotional classic *The Imitation of Christ,* the fifteenth-century spiritual writer Thomas à Kempis defined contemplation as a "familiar friendship with Jesus."[52]

You can be friends with Jesus. Like Mary who "sat at the Lord's feet listening to what he said,"[53] you can sit before Jesus daily, letting him speak to you, teach you, direct you, and, above all, love you. This is "the life that is truly life."

If this isn't your experience of prayer—if for you prayer is closer to boredom, distraction, and scary emotions coming to the surface of your heart—please don't shame yourself or self-flagellate; that won't help.

Just keep praying.

Stay with it. The one non-negotiable rule of prayer is this: *Keep showing up.* Stay with the process until you experience what all the fuss is about. Don't stop until you know by direct experience what I'm stumbling to name with words.

For years, when I read about monks and nuns who gave up a "normal" life to do little else besides pray, I'd think they were a little crazy. (For the record, some of them *were,* and some more than a little.) But what if *we're* the ones who are unhinged? We who would rather binge Netflix or go shopping or play fantasy football than commune with Love loving? Who would rather give the vast majority of our time to slaving away for some job that will chew us up and spit us out the moment we're no longer useful to the bottom line? Who choose to spend hours every day on our phones yet claim we "don't have time" for God? What if *we're* the ones who have lost touch with reality? Who are wasting our lives on trivial things?

Is your heart waking up yet?

Is there a flame down in your soul starting to burn with desire for friendship with Jesus? If so, let me offer you hope: You can "take hold of the life that is truly life," the life Jesus died to make possible.[54]

Here's a good place to start: Go and find what Jesus called "the secret place" . . .

Find your secret place

Jesus said something about prayer that I find surprising (which is *not* surprising). His first piece of advice was not about *what* to pray but *where:*

> When you pray, go into your room, and when you have shut your door, pray to your Father who is in the secret place; and your Father who sees in secret will reward you openly.[55]

The word Jesus used for "room" is *tameion* in Greek, and it can also be translated "inner room."[56] Within a typical first-century Galilean home was an inner room, kind of like a closet or pantry, used to store foodstuffs and supplies. Most of life was spent outdoors, so the home was mostly for sleeping and storage. Jesus' advice was to go hide in the *tameion* and there, "in secret," pray.

I'm writing this book from a little office in an Oregon forest. It's quiet, and the only distractions are those I brought in my own mind. Why here and not on a street corner downtown? Because I'm a *person,* in a body, and environment matters. Certain environments help me focus on my work, while others sabotage my best intentions.

In the same way, if we want to reach the depth of life with God that Jesus modeled, we need to find a diversion-free place to get away and be alone with the Father. It could be an office in the woods, your bedroom late at night, or a park down the street from your house. Or if all else fails, a closet or pantry.

The point is that, like Jesus, we need to learn to hide.

When you read the four biographies of Jesus in the New Testament, one thing is painfully clear: Jesus' life template was based on a rhythm of *retreat* and *return*, like breathing in and then out. Jesus would retreat: He would slip away from the noise and press of the crowd and find a place where he could pray, alone or sometimes with a few very close friends. He would inhale. Then he would exhale, or return: He would come back to preach and teach and heal and deliver and offer love. In Mark 1, we read,

> Very early in the morning, while it was still dark, Jesus got up, left the house and went off to a solitary place, where he prayed.[57]

The phrase "solitary place" is one word in Greek: *erēmos*. It can be translated "deserted place," "lonely place," or "quiet place."[58] In Luke 5, we read the same word again:

> Jesus often withdrew to lonely places [*erēmos*] and prayed.[59]

Notice, he *often* withdrew to the *erēmos*. On the night before his arrest, Jesus went to Gethsemane, a park outside the city of Jerusalem. The writer Luke tells us he went there "as usual."[60] One version has "as was His *habit*."[61] And the writer John added that the betrayer Judas knew to go there "because Jesus had *often* met there with his disciples."[62]

For Jesus, the secret place wasn't just a place; it was a *practice,* a habit, a part of his life rhythm. He seemed to have little hiding places all over Israel where he would slip away to pray.

This practice from the life of Jesus has come to be called "the spiritual discipline of solitude, silence, and stillness." And no matter your personality type, whether you are a thinker or more of a doer, an introvert craving time alone or an extrovert ready to party "all day every day, baby," this practice is absolutely vital to your spiritual life. Henri Nouwen once said, bluntly but accurately,

> Without solitude it is virtually impossible to live a spiritual life.[63]

There's a legendary story about Nouwen going to ask Mother Teresa for spiritual direction (to be a fly on *that* wall . . .). Her advice was spartan: "Spend one hour a day in adoration of your Lord and never do anything that you know is wrong."[64]

For many of you, an hour a day may be unrealistic.[65] But could you do a half hour? Twenty minutes? Surely you could begin with ten?

We all have excuses for why it's hard to make time to pray, but many of them are just that—excuses. A push-pull dynamic is at work within *all* our hearts (myself included). Part of us deeply desires God, and part of us resists him and wants to rule over our own kingdoms, thank you very much.

But one reason so many people avoid the quiet is just because they have yet to find a way of being with God that is conducive to their personalities and stages of life. Yes, I'm an introvert. No, I don't have little kids anymore. Yes, I live in a house, not a tiny apartment. But I think of my friend Tyler[66] who is nothing like me—full-tilt extrovert, action oriented, father to three young boys. He goes to bed early and gets up every single day at five A.M. (because it's the only time he's not needed); he goes outside, prays a psalm on his porch, then goes prayer walking in a park across the street. He does this *all* year long, including all through the Portland winter. "The cold just makes me feel so alive," he confided in me (when I asked if he was crazy).

Tyler and I have very different personalities, but we share an ache for God and we have both come to love prayer. I do it sitting cross-legged in the quiet of my room; he does it walking in a city park in a raincoat. Different method, same goal.

When the secret place is turned into a preference-based devotional option for introverted intellectuals, it's a great tragedy—similar to how in the Middle Ages a serious pursuit of Jesus was perceived as only for monks and nuns, not ordinary people. It's a tragedy for extroverts because they never reach the depth of life with Jesus that is on offer. And it's a tragedy for introverts, too, because a spiritual discipline that was designed to free us from ourselves and form us into people of self-giving love is twisted into "a little me time for Dad to recharge," which often does nothing but deepen our bondage to self, not liberate it.

So, work *with* your personality, not against it; tailor your practice to your Myers-Briggs type and stage of life, but *find your secret place.* Go there as often as you can. Prioritize it. Fall in love with it, with God. Without quiet prayer, your life with God will wither; with it, you will come alive to the greatest joy of life: a familiar friendship to Jesus.

"You must ruthlessly eliminate hurry from your life"

Yes, this sounds like a lot. But let me make one thing perfectly clear: The call to apprentice under Jesus is a call not to do *more* but to do *less*.

It's not addition but subtraction.

It's not about increasing complexity but about pursuing simplicity.

It's less about "habit stacking"[67] than it is about learning to say *no*.

Jesus is calling you to slow down and simplify your life around the three goals of an apprentice: To be with your rabbi, become like him, and do as he did. To make apprenticeship to him the animating center of gravity for your entire life.

The elephant in the room is that the vast majority of us have far too much going on to "add" Jesus into our overly busy schedules. I'm so sorry, but I don't know how to soften the blow: There is simply no way to follow Jesus without unhurrying your life.

Dallas Willard famously called hurry "the great enemy of spiritual life in our day" and said, "You must ruthlessly eliminate hurry from your life."[68] Hurry is, arguably, the *number one* challenge you will face should you decide to take following Jesus seriously. Like an enemy, it won't just stand in your way; it will actively fight *against* you.

The nonprofit I currently run started as a five-year spiritual formation initiative at Bridgetown Church that we called "Practicing the Way." Before we began, I sat down with a psychologist who is one of the smartest Christians I know to get constructive criticism on our vision for a new kind of church. He mostly confirmed that our ideas were well grounded in both Scripture and science and gave his blessing. But he buffered it with this ominous warning: "The number one problem you will face is *time,*" he said, because "most people are just too busy to live emotionally healthy and spiritually vibrant lives."[69]

We live time-torn lives: We *want* to be with Jesus, but we just don't have time to pray. We genuinely desire to grow into people of love, but our to-do lists are too long to make any serious attempt. We know rest is the secret to the spiritual journey, but Sabbath? That's one-seventh of our lives! And yet we are totally unsatisfied: We feel hurried, anxious, far from God, spiritually shallow, and stuck in our self-defeating habits of behavior. The spiritual journey to reach the heights of the kingdom has hit a plateau; the Way has become a loop; Easter has become Groundhog Day.

We just can't keep living like this. As Rich Villodas, a pastor in New York City, put it in his book *The Deeply Formed Life,*

> Our souls were not created for the kind of speed to which we have grown accustomed. Thus, we are a people who are out of rhythm, a people with too much to do and not enough time to do it. . . .
> Our lives can easily take us to the brink of burnout. The pace we live at is often destructive. The lack of

margin is debilitating. We are worn out. In all of this, the problem before us is not just the frenetic pace we live at but what gets pushed out from our lives as a result; that is, *life with God*.[70]

So, this will require us to take intentional steps to slow down.[71] It will likely start with a formation audit[72] of our lives, where we take a serious look at how we spend our time and *cut out* more than we *add in,* in a desire to be with Jesus.

This may sound like no fun at all, but it's good news—the best of news. Jesus is not a recruiter for WeWork, calling us to "hustle harder," but the good shepherd of Psalm 23, calling us to "lie down in green pastures."

When Jesus said, "Come, follow me," he was simultaneously saying there are some things we all must leave behind. "Take up your cross" was a way of saying that sacrifice is required. There are things we must die to, release, let go.

Ronald Rolheiser has said, "Every choice is a thousand renunciations."[73] Meaning, every *yes* is a thousand *nos*. To say yes to Jesus' invitation to apprentice under him is to say *no* to countless other invitations.

I've literally quit my job (twice now) in large part to live a slower, simpler life. So far, my only regret is that I didn't do it sooner. Hopefully, this will not require you to quit your job, but it may. For most of us, it will just require us to cancel a few digital subscriptions, apologetically bow out of a few obligations, watch less TV, go to bed earlier (to get up and pray), and just make space in our days to pause, to breathe, to abide.

Why not unhurry your life to apprentice under Jesus?

Why not utilize the practices of Jesus (which we'll cover later in the book) to slow down your mind and body, to gaze at the beauty of God—to look at Jesus, looking at you, in love? Surely practicing this Way must be better than how you are currently living. Why not just *try* it?

In John 1, Jesus said to a few potential disciples, "Come and see."[74] Meaning, "Come and live the Way with me for a while, and see whether life together in the kingdom of love is not far better than *any* other kingdom, whether this path is not better than any other path."

Come and see . . .

Practicing the Way—

Goal #2: Become like him

The skull.

It's staring at me now, its hollow eye sockets boring into my soul, refusing to let me avoid the ultimate human reality: *death*.

It could be half a century from now or half an hour, but I am going to die, as are you. The stats are pretty compelling: near 100 percent. The reaper is coming for us all.

Hence the skull on my office desk.

No, no, it's not real; no need to call a mental health professional.[1] But still, it calls for a little backstory . . .

In the sixth century, a monk named Benedict wrote the now famous *Rule of St. Benedict,* the founding document of one of the oldest monastic orders in the world. In it, he gave this advice to his fellow monks:

Day by day remind yourself that you are going to die.

Does this sound a bit masochistic to your modern ears? I imagine, yes. But in context, Benedict was essentially saying, "*Don't waste your life on triviality.* Remember what matters. Life is fleeting and precious. Don't squander it. Keep your death before your eyes. Hold eternity in your heart." Benedict was urging the monks to be joyfully present to the miracle of daily life.

Long before the skull was the trademark aesthetic of punk rock bands, motorcycle gangs, or Hollywood pirates, it was the visual motif of Christian monks. For centuries, monks would go into their cells and kneel on prayer benches with three items spread before them: a portion of Scripture, a candle (to read said Scripture), and a skull. Not a skull bought on Etsy, as mine is, but a *real* one—likely from a previous denizen of the monastery: "my old roommate, Brother Makarios."

The skull was a daily reminder that *life is fleeting; don't miss it.*

To this day, Benedictine monks wear black robes—not because they are trying to be chic but because they view the life of discipleship as a kind of preparation for death, for an eternity with God.

Benedictine monasteries often have their own cemeteries, as their monks take vows of stability and pledge to remain in the community until their death. Certain monasteries intentionally leave the next grave pre-dug, so that every day, as the monks walk by the plot, they remember, *I'm going to join my brothers soon.*

Archaeologists have even discovered ancient catacombs with this saying carved into the wall above the ossuary:

What you are now, we used to be.
What we are now, you will be.

So, the skull. On my desk. My attempt to remind myself I'm going to die.

It's there because in any age, but especially in ours, it's incredibly easy to *waste* our lives. "Amusing ourselves to death," as the social critic Neil Postman called it, has never been more convenient.[3] You can disappear into the black hole of Netflix, become a workaholic in pursuit of riches or fame, or simply "eat, drink, and be merry" in the adult playground of the modern city. Western culture is arguably built around the denial of death through the coping mechanism of distraction. As Ronald Rolheiser put it, "We are distracting ourselves into spiritual oblivion."[4]

But—not to put a damper on things—you will eventually die. We *all* will. And when that day comes and your friends and family stand around your grave, what will matter most is who you *became*.

New York Times columnist David Brooks famously distinguished between "résumé virtues" and "eulogy virtues."[5] Résumé virtues are what we talk about in life—where we work, what we've accomplished, what accolades we've received, and so on. Eulogy virtues are what *others* talk about when we *die*—namely, the people we were, the fabric that made up our character, and the relationships that defined our sojourn on this earth.

To "remind yourself that you are going to die" is to remind yourself to live for your eulogy, not your résumé. It's to not waste your precious, fleeting time here but to focus on what matters in the grand scheme of eternity—becoming a person of love through union with Jesus.

Benedict was an apprentice of Jesus who, in time, became a bona fide saint. Like a true apprentice, he saw our years in the body as a kind of training ground for eternity. That ultimately, what we're learning is how to become a person of love, a person who is like Jesus.

Now we're to goal #2 of an apprentice: Become *like* Jesus.

To recap, the aim of a first-century apprentice wasn't just to learn the Torah from a smart rabbi, but to learn *life* from one who had become a master of it. We see this in Jesus' rubric:

> The apprentice is not above the rabbi, but everyone who is fully trained will be *like* their rabbi.[6]

For Jesus, the point of apprenticeship was to be *with* him for the purpose of becoming *like* him, which happens through an in-depth process of training. Apprentices of Jesus are those who sign up for this training program, who intentionally arrange their lives around this goal of spiritual growth and maturity.

(Again, non-apprentices of Jesus are those who intentionally arrange their lives around anything *else*.)

The monks have long called this process *imitatio Christi,* or "the imitation of Christ." Today we call it "spiritual formation."

Spiritual formation isn't a Christian thing

Here's the *first* thing you need to understand about spiritual formation, and it's key: *Spiritual formation isn't a Christian thing; it's a human thing.*

To be human is to change, constantly. Whether we are religious or not, we grow, evolve, fall apart, and come back together. We can't help it; the nature of the human soul is dynamic, not static. It's why we show awkward teenager photos at weddings and wedding photos at funerals—we're all fascinated by this process of change.

At the risk of saying it yet *again,* the question isn't, Are you being formed? It's, *Who* or *what* are you being formed *into?*

Who we are—the good, bad, and ugly—is *all* a result of spiritual formation. I occasionally hear people say they are "getting into spiritual formation," by which they usually mean they are beginning to practice spiritual disciplines, read books, and possibly doing the "work" in therapy. All very good. But to clarify, you've been being spiritually formed since before you came out of your mother's womb. All of us have.

Spiritual formation happens to everyone, whether they are "into" it or not. Mother Teresa was a product of spiritual formation, and so was Hitler. Gandhi was spiritually formed, as was Chairman Mao. Same with Michelle Obama, Lady Gaga, Brené Brown, or Volodymyr Zelenskyy. Their spirits have been formed over a long period of time through a complex alchemy of genetic inheritance, family patterns, childhood wounds, education, habits, decisions, relationships, inner orientations, attitudes, environments, responses to said environments, and more.

Same with *all* of us.

You've *been* formed already.

You're *being* formed even now as you read.

You *will be* formed in days to come.

Put another way, *you're becoming a person.*[7]

The question Saint Benedict would have us sit with is this: *Who am I becoming?*

Spiritual formation is *not* optional. Every thought you think, every emotion you let shape your behavior, every attitude you let rest in your body, every decision you make, each word you speak, every relationship you enter into, the habits that make up your days, whether or not you have social media (if you do, how you use it), how you respond to pain and suffering, how you handle failure or success—*all* these things and more are forming us into a particular shape.[8] Stasis is not on the menu. We are being either transformed into the love and beauty of Jesus or malformed by the entropy of sin and death. "We become either agents of God's healing and liberating grace, or carriers of the sickness of the world."[9] To believe otherwise is an illusion; and to give no thought to this is to come dangerously close to wasting your life.

Writing about hell, C. S. Lewis claimed that *all* of us are on a trajectory to either life or death, and the farther we follow that trajectory, the more pronounced its effect on us becomes. He said we are either becoming "immortal horrors or everlasting splendours."[10] Willard argued that death just seals the trajectory of the road, or "way," we chose in life.[11] It's clear that some people are living in hell *now,* while others are living in a kind of heaven on earth.

We're not all following the same path.

Case in point: elderly people. Most people over the age of eighty are either the *best* or the *worst* people you know. Hear me; I do *not* mean this in an ageist way. Just the opposite, in fact. Most twentysomethings I know are just kind of *mid,* as my teenage kids would say. They aren't saints or potential terrorists; they're just normal. This *isn't* true of most elderly people I know. Run through your mental Rolodex of people past eighty: Most of them are either the most gracious, happy, grateful, patient, loving, self-giving people you know, just happy to be alive and sitting in the room with you, *or* the most bitter, manipulative, spiteful people you know, oozing emotional poison into their family lines and reveling in others' pain. Sure, some are in the middle of the bell curve, but most are noticeably to one side.

That's because they've spent almost a century *becoming a person.* Being formed. Through some strange, invisible chemical reaction of habits, mindsets, chosen attitudes, life circumstances, suffering, successes, failures, and random events, they became who they are.

This is spiritual formation.

Formation defined

Now, let's define spiritual formation in the Way of *Jesus.*

If spiritual formation is simply the way the human spirit, or self, is formed into a definitive shape (for better or worse), then spiritual formation in the Way of Jesus is how each of us is formed to be like *Jesus* and, in doing so, to be our deepest, truest self—the self that God had in mind when he willed us into existence before time began.

The irony of our "be true to yourself" culture is that everyone ends up looking the *same.* As it turns out, sin is incredibly cliché.

We devolve to our base animal instincts for self-preservation and pleasure—greed, gluttony, immorality, lies, power games. It's the same story on repeat, from Homer's *The Iliad* to the morning news.

A true original is one practicing the Way.

Because no one is more original than a saint.

With that in mind, let me attempt a working definition of spiritual formation in the Way of Jesus: *the process of being formed into people of love in Christ.*

Let's parse this out.

"The process"

Formation into the image of Jesus is a long, *slow* process, not a one-time event. There's no lightning bolt from heaven. Spiritual growth is similar to bodily growth—very gradual. It takes place over a lifetime at an incremental, at times imperceptible rate. Yes, we experience periods of dramatic change like birth or a teenage growth spurt, but those key inflection points are the exceptions, not the rule.

As the Regent College professor James Houston often said, "Spiritual formation is the slowest of all human movements."

This is a provocative challenge to our instant-gratification culture; we're used to fast and faster—the entire world just a swipe of our thumb away. Click the button and have it delivered within hours. But the formation of the human soul doesn't work at digital speed.

If we lose sight of this—and I'm speaking to myself here as much as to you, channeling the skull two feet away—we will either grow discouraged and give up, or settle for mediocre. "Christians aren't perfect, just forgiven."[12] (As if the best we can hope for is a little tune-up on the way to the afterlife.) But we cannot lower the horizon of possibility that was set by the extraordinary life of Jesus and gift of his Spirit. Instead, we must stay with the process for as long as it takes to actualize our destinies.

And this may take a very long time.

Recently I was venting to my wife about how discouraged I was over my lifelong struggle with anxiety. I *hate* how stressed I get at times and how my mind will get stuck in an all-too-familiar loop of negative rumination.

"Do you think I will ever mature beyond this?" I asked her.

"Of course," she said. "I'm positive. I think you'll become deeply happy and calm."

"Really? How much longer?" I wondered out loud.

"I'd guess in your sixties," she said, deadpan.

She wasn't trying to be funny; that was her best estimate. And she's likely right.

The spiritual teacher Pete Scazzero once told me a maxim that was passed on to him by an older, wiser mentor: "The best decade of your life will be your seventies, the second best will be your eighties, and the third will be your sixties." By *best* he did not mean the happiest (though I expect that too) but our richest and most joyful and helpful to others.

Don't get me wrong; there's *joy* to be had *all along the way.* You could argue that joy is the defining feature of a life organized around God. But it's rarely the explosive happiness of an emotional high, dramatic yet fickle and fleeting. It's more like a quiet undercurrent that slowly accumulates at the base of your soul, increasingly welling up like a soft melody that over the years becomes the soundtrack of your life.

But. It's a process.

"Of being formed"

Formation into the image of Jesus isn't something we *do* as much as it's something that is done *to* us, by God himself, as we yield to his work of transforming grace. Our job is mostly to make ourselves available.

Pick your analogy from Scripture: We're the sheep, he's the shepherd; we're the clay, he's the potter; we're the child in utero, he's the mother, laboring in the pains of childbirth.[13]

This doesn't mean we're off the hook—"Let go and let God." No, we have a responsibility to cooperate with God's transforming grace. He won't force it on us. As Saint Augustine said in the fourth century,

> Without God, we cannot.
> Without us, God will not.

Much of Christians' current disillusionment over their lack of transformation is because they have never learned *their* part in spiritual formation. But our job isn't to self-save; it's to surrender.

One of the many gifts of the addiction community has been its unsparing honesty about just how weak and in need of grace and community we *all* are, and just how inept our willpower is.[14] When AA (which started out as a discipleship program) translated the language of God into a "Higher Power," they were acknowledging that we need a power far greater than ourselves to get free. We who got ourselves into this mess can't get ourselves out. We're too broken to put ourselves back together. Too lost to find ourselves. When we unmask the human facade of self-delusion, we realize just how utterly unlike Christ we are in the deepest recesses of our hearts. We are forced to confront our *true* natures—how warped and wounded we really are. In that tender place, we all realize, *I can't self-save*. "Physician, heal thyself" is a strategy doomed to fail. We need help, power, from beyond us. We need grace.

Formation isn't a Christianized version of project self; it's a process of salvation. Of *being* saved by Jesus.

"Into people of love"

An apprentice of Jesus is one who has arranged their life around becoming like Jesus, as expressed through their personality, gender, life stage, culture, ethnicity, and so on. But if you had to summarize Christlike character in one word, there would be no competition: *love*.

Love is the acid test of spiritual formation.

The single most important question is, Are we becoming more loving? Not, Are we becoming more biblically educated? Or practicing more spiritual disciplines? Or more involved in church? Those are all good things, but not the most important thing.

If you want to chart your progress on the spirituality journey, test the quality of your closest relationships—namely, by love and the fruit of the Spirit. Would the people who know you best say you are becoming more loving, joyful, and at peace? More patient and less frustrated? Kinder, gentler, softening with time, and pervaded by goodness? Faithful, especially in hard times, and self-controlled?

Are you growing in love not just for your friends and family but for your enemies? When you are hurt, wounded, and treated unjustly (as we all are), are you finding yourself increasingly able to emotionally release the bitterness, to absorb the pain and not give it back in kind? To pray for and even "bless those who curse you"[15]?

And is all this feeling more and more natural and less forced? More and more like this is just who you *are*?

If not, then no matter how well you know the Bible, how many books you read, how many insights you amass, or how many practices you build into your Rule of Life, you're not on track.

Because the telos of the spiritual journey is to become like God, and "God is love."[16] Remember Saint Ignatius's insight that God is "Love loving"? Love isn't just something God does; it's *who he is*. He can't help but love; it's his nature. Some of us are amazed that Jesus doesn't hate us for all our flaws and failures, but that just betrays our distorted vision of God. It would be much harder for God to hate us than to love us, because *love is who God is inside his deepest self.*

This is why God is Trinity (more on this coming soon): because God is love and love cannot exist outside relationship. Ergo, God *must* be a kind of relationship—one that is self-giving, others centered, humble, and joyful and full of blessing and goodwill. To quote Saint Augustine yet again, "God is (at once) Lover, Beloved, and Love itself."[17] He is the one who loves, the one who is loved, and the ultimate source of all love.

And remember, love as defined by Jesus is not just a nice feeling of affection. It's an attitude, yes, of compassion, warmth, and delight, but it's also an *action*. It's *agape*—to will the good of another *ahead* of your own, no matter the cost or sacrifice that may require. As Jesus said, "Greater love has no one than this: to lay down one's life for one's friends."[18] It's the cross. Which isn't just something Jesus did for us; it's *also* something we do *with* him: "This is how we know what love is: Jesus Christ laid down his life for us. And we ought to lay down our lives for our brothers and sisters."[19]

This is where spiritual formation veers in a wildly different direction from the self-actualization movement or the Western obsession with project self: It has an end goal, a telos—it's designed to form you into a person of *agape*.

The professor Dr. Robert Mulholland defines spiritual formation as "a process of being formed into the image of Christ for the sake of others"[20] and *harps* on the "for the sake of others" piece. Without this crucial element, formation will inevitably devolve into a private, therapeutic self-help spirituality that is, honestly, just a Christianized version of radical individualism, not a crucible to burn our souls clean and forge us into people of love like Jesus.

Yes, there is a journey inward and even a self-discovery that are key to Christian spirituality, but it's followed by a journey *outward* into love—into *action* in the world. The goal is to be formed by Jesus, at every level of our beings, into those who are pervaded by love.

But again, we *cannot* do this alone. There is only one way . . .

"In Christ"

Christlikeness is the result of Christ *in* us. It's all grace; it's always been grace. "Christ *in* you, the hope of glory."[21] And us *in* Christ. In fact, "in Christ" is a phrase used all through the New Testament, more than eighty times in Paul's letters alone. Theologians call this doctrine "incorporation"—being incorporated, integrated into the inner life of God himself through Christ. Jesus has come to draw us *into* God's inner life of Love loving. As the pastor Darrell Johnson put it in his book on the Trinity, to experience this is "to be alive in the intimacy at the center of the universe."[22] As Jesus said in John 17, right before his death,

> I pray also for those who will believe in me . . . that all of them may be one, Father, just as you are in me and I am in you. May they also be in us . . . I in them and you in me—so that they may be brought to complete unity. Then the world will know that you sent me and have loved them even as you have loved me.[23]

This is the gospel: God has drawn near to us in Jesus—*us,* we who are sinful, broken, wounded, mortal, dying, and incapable of self-saving, with many of us completely uninterested in God or even enemies of God—to draw *us* into his inner life, to heal us by immersing us within the fold of his Trinitarian love, and then to send us out into the world as agents of his love.

Jesus' invitation to apprentice under him isn't just a chance to become people of love who are *like* God; it's a chance to enter the inner life of God himself. The ancients called this "union" with God, and it is *the very meaning of our human existence*—for me and for every human on the planet, whether they realize and receive it or not.

This, then, is spiritual formation: *the process of being formed into a person of self-giving love through deepening surrender to and union with the Trinity.*

You're becoming a person; that much is unavoidable.

And you're going to end up *somewhere* in life.

Why not become a person who is pervaded by the love of Jesus?

Why not end up in union with God?

No accidental saints

Here's the thing: As great as this sounds, it isn't going to just magically happen.

Christlikeness is possible, but it's not natural.

In fact, the gravity and inertia of life will likely take you in the *opposite* direction. "Small is the gate and narrow the road that leads to life, and only a few find it," as Jesus said.[24]

Put another way, there are no accidental saints.

Nobody wakes up one morning around age fifty and thinks, *Wow, would you look at that? I became a saint. Weird.* Or *Hmm, it seems I've been living the Sermon on the Mount. I'm increasingly free of all worry, care, judgmentalism, lust, and anger; money no longer has a hold on my heart; I'm no longer run by fear and the need to look good to other people; I feel free; I've been pervaded by love, even love for my enemies. What a nice coincidence.*

Yeah . . . *no.*

Formation *will* happen to you, per our earlier argument, with zero conscious decision on your part, but formation *into a person of love in Christ* will *not.* That you must choose, and keep choosing, day after day. It will require an intentionality. You will have to apprentice under Jesus and follow his process of training.[25]

"Yes," you say, "I'm in, but I'm not sure where to start."

If that's your heart, you're not alone. But tragically, many people genuinely *want* to apprentice under Jesus, but they don't know *how.* Spiritual formation in the North American church is often truncated to this three-part formula:

1. Go to church.

2. Read your Bible and pray.

3. Give.

I'm *all* for these three practices (all three are in my Rule of Life). But in my experience, many Christians get thirty years down the road with this as their template for discipleship and don't feel all that different; they just feel *older.*

Dr. Janet Hagberg and Robert Guelich from Fuller Seminary spent decades analyzing the data of thousands of Christians' lives, searching for a developmental process by which we become more like Jesus over our lifetimes. They identified a six-stage spiritual development theory:[26]

The Critical Journey

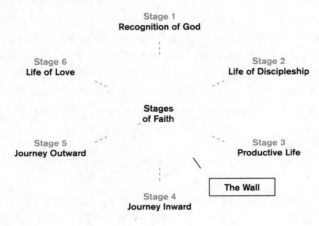

Stage 1
Recognition of God

Stage 6
Life of Love

Stage 2
Life of Discipleship

Stages of Faith

Stage 5
Journey Outward

Stage 3
Productive Life

The Wall

Stage 4
Journey Inward

After watching this process unfold over many lives, they made this sobering observation: Most Christians never mature beyond stage three, which is a very basic level of maturity; *very few* reach their full potential in Christ.[27]

There are lots of reasons for this,[28] but one is pragmatic: Most people do not have a working theory of change; meaning, *a reliable path of transformation to follow.*

In both my personal and pastoral experience, the problem is not that people don't want to change (most do) or aren't trying to change (most are); it's that they do not know *how* to change. We don't have a good grasp on how the human soul goes from spiritual birth to spiritual maturity. So we have a lot of spiritual adolescents, but few elders.

Years ago, I had the chance to attend Richard Foster's last public event. In the late seventies, Foster wrote a book called *Celebration of Discipline* that sold over a million copies (with the word *discipline* in the title!) and arguably inspired the renaissance of the spiritual formation movement in the Western, Protestant stream of the church. Sitting in on his final public teaching was a holy moment for me. Richard is a true sage. And after decades of traveling all over the world teaching on spiritual formation, he lovingly concluded that most people "had no theology of spiritual growth." He was struck by "the abysmal ignorance people have of *how* we are transformed." He said this with zero judgment, only grief.

Very few people have even thought that deeply about it at all.

As a result, most people's theories of change tend to be

- Unconscious, not conscious

- Haphazard, not intentional

- Secular, not scriptural

- Mostly ineffective, not transformational

The fallout of this ignorance is several well-known phenomena across the Western church:

- Churches full of people who are Christians but not apprentices of Jesus

- A widespread cancer of hypocrisy that has infected the church, where the gap between Jesus' teachings and people's day-to-day lives (including those of many pastors) is too great to be explained away graciously

- A generation of people disillusioned with the faith, with a million millennials leaving the church each year and many even giving up on following Jesus entirely, looking instead to quasi-scientific therapeutic strategies of self-help or Eastern religions as more-promising options for salvation

 - Many who quietly ache for more of God and his transformation but feel stuck on their spiritual journeys and blocked in their growth

This isn't to critique, judge, or indict *anyone*. It's to name what *is*. Many of us simply have not been taught a Jesus-based model of change, an effective pathway to transformation, a *way* of life.

Or worse . . . we *have* been taught, but poorly.

Three losing strategies

To become like Jesus, we need a working theory of change that . . . well, *works*.

Let's start with what *doesn't* work (we'll get to what does soon). I have repeatedly seen three losing strategies in my twenty-plus years as a pastor.

Losing strategy #1: Willpower

The problem with willpower isn't that it's bad (it's not); it just doesn't work very well. We all know the stat: 80 percent of New Year's resolutions fail by the end of January.[29] That's because willpower is a finite resource; we only have so much of it each day. (Mine is normally used up by about noon.) It's like a muscle. Not only does it tap out after overuse, but even at its best, it's rarely strong enough for any kind of heavy lifting.

Small changes, like beginning your day by reading a psalm or cussing less, are usually within the realm of willpower. However, within you and all around you are strong forces that eat willpower for breakfast: deeply ingrained habits of sin that come from your family line, the automatic responses of your body, and any form of trauma, addiction, or fear.

The genius of Jesus' ethical teaching was that you cannot keep the law by trying not to break the law. You cannot become more loving by *trying* to become more loving, no matter how much self-effort you bring to the table. You have to be transformed in your inner person, or what Jesus called "the heart."

This isn't to negate the role of self-effort: *Self-effort is key to spiritual formation.* There is a synergistic relationship between our spirits, or willpower, and God's Spirit, or power. Self-effort and grace are partners, not competitors locked in a tug-of-war for glory. But the main function of self-effort in our formation is to do what we *can* do—make space to surrender to God via the practices of Jesus—so God can do what we *can't* do: heal, liberate, and transform us into people of love.

As Leslie Jamison said in her memoir about recovering from addiction, "I needed to believe in something stronger than my willpower."[30]

Willpower is crucial, but it's not the solution.

Losing strategy #2: More Bible study

A lot of churches operate on the assumption that as a person's knowledge of the Bible increases, their maturity will increase with it. I have been around Bible-teaching churches for my entire life, and I can *assure* you this is, at best, wildly insufficient.

Protestants (rightly, I think) emphasize the formative power of Scripture to shape us into the mold of Jesus. "All Scripture is God breathed and is *useful* . . ."[31] Jesus himself was a rabbi; his teaching was saturated in Scripture to the nth degree. But we Protestants are easily blinded by other Western assumptions, such as René Descartes's famous claim, "I think; therefore I am." We can easily fall into a thoroughly unbiblical view of the human soul as a kind of brain on legs. As Thomas Edison once said, "The chief function of the body is to carry the brain around."

But the philosopher James K. A. Smith said it well: "You can't think your way to Christlikeness."[32] Because, again, practicing the Way of Jesus is less like learning quantum physics and more like learning aikido. It's something you *do* with your whole body. Love isn't an intellectual theory; it's an embodied way of being.

This is why information alone does not produce transformation. Because *knowing* something is not the same as *doing* something, which is still not the same as *becoming* the kind of person who does something naturally as a by-product of a transformed inner nature.

Example: Do any of you struggle with anxiety or fear? I do. I'm guessing that you, like me, know that Jesus commands you to not fear. Your problem (and mine) isn't a lack of information or even a lack of inspiration—we *all* desire to be free of fear. It's the problem of how to get what you *already know* and *deeply desire* into your central nervous system, how to overcome habits of fear that are woven into your body's neurobiology.

Or let's take another example: generosity. If you gave a pop quiz to every single Christian on earth and asked, "Does God call you to be generous?" *100 percent* would say yes. So, why aren't more of us generous? The problem isn't that we don't know the right answer; it's that Jesus' teachings on money and generosity have yet to get into the deepest parts of our beings.[33]

My point is that church attendance, good sermons, and regular Bible study are all good—more than good, *essential.* But we must be honest: *By themselves,* they have a very poor track record of yielding a high level of transformation in large numbers of people.

Losing strategy #3: The zap from heaven

I call this one "the Matrix theory of spiritual formation." Remember the scene in the original Matrix movie where Neo and Trinity are trapped on the roof? (Yes, *that* scene.) They need an escape route, and there's a helicopter, but Trinity doesn't know how to fly it. *No problemo* in the Matrix. She calls the operator: "Tank, I need a pilot program for a B-21-2 helicopter—hurry!" You see her eyes flutter, and then, *boom,* she can fly a helicopter. They elude Mr. Smith with ease.

That's how many people approach spiritual formation: waiting for a "download" from heaven to radically change them in an instant.

At its best, this is a rightfully high view of the power of the Holy Spirit to deeply change us through encounter with him. To break strongholds over our lives, heal our memories, rewire our nervous systems, and touch our bodies. I'd go so far as to say any theory of change that *doesn't* incorporate the need for moments of breakthrough will have only limited results.

But at its worst, this is laziness, pure and simple, because it's far easier to go to church once a week chasing a spiritual high and angle for a download from heaven than to do the daily, unglamorous work of discipleship. This approach can be just another search for a quick fix, a shortcut, what the psychologist John Welwood called "spiritual bypassing"—trying to skip over our pain and just have Jesus "fix" us. Cue the rise of conference junkies chasing the next spiritual high or people who show up at church *every* time the doors are open but refuse to go to therapy.

Jesus *is* in the business of healing souls. But while the four Gospels have dozens of stories of Jesus instantly healing people's *bodies* (after which, by the way, he almost always gave them instructions to go and *do* something as a next step), he doesn't seem to do the same with people's *characters*. There is *not a single instance* in which he simply waved his hand to take away an ugly habit or personality trait in one of his apprentices. The opposite is true—we see their stubborn sinfulness live on for years. Jesus didn't zap them; he just kept teaching, rebuking, and loving them, giving them time to grow and mature.

Interesting

Miracles, emotional breakthroughs, and profound moments of radical change *do* happen, and *need* to happen, but they are not the daily path of discipleship. Like growth spurts or invasive surgeries in a child or adolescent, they are an essential part of our development as persons, but *most* of our growth is a slow, incremental but noticeable maturation into adulthood.

A lightning bolt from heaven is not (likely) the solution.

To reiterate, *all* three of these strategies highlight something key: the centrality of our will, the key role of Scripture, and our need for encounter. Yet in isolation, they don't seem to work nearly as well as you'd think.

Why is that?

Two problems . . .

Problem #1: Sin

The first is what we Christians call "sin."

I recognize that a growing number of people have an emotional allergy to the word *sin,* but it is just the word we use to name the felt experience of the human condition that pretty much *all* luminary thinkers agree on. Whether ancient, modern, Eastern, Western, religious, or secular, they all harmonize on this specific point: Something is deeply *off* in the human heart.

It's not just that we do terrible things; it's worse——we often _want_ to do terrible things. And even when we *don't* want to do terrible things, we still get pulled into doing them, like a drug addict caught in a self-defeating loop.

The New Testament writers speak of sin as not just an action, but also a condition—of being *in sin*. We screw up, we offend, we hurt, we betray, we forget, we say things we regret. "To err is human." Calling people "sinful" is no more judgmental than a doctor telling a patient they have a liver condition. It's just honest.

To make progress in our formation, we *must* face our sin. Otherwise, the spiritual journey is like trying to run an ultramarathon with a broken leg and stage IV cancer. Good luck.

Now, stay with me for a few minutes because this next part is key for you to understand. In biblical theology, there are three dimensions to sin:

#1 Sin done *by* us

This is the most obvious. Repeat what I just said: We muck things up. We forget to call home on Mother's Day; we have an affair; we disparage our children; we make excuses rather than apologize; we lie to save face; we _____.

Francis Spufford, the irreverent but witty author of *Unapologetic: Why, Despite Everything, Christianity Can Still Make Surprising Emotional Sense,* called it "HPTMTU"—shorthand for "the human propensity to muck things up." (Only he didn't use the word *muck*.)[34]

#2 Sin done *to* us

But sin done by us is not the only dimension. We've all been hurt, wounded, slighted, betrayed, abandoned, treated unjustly, falsely accused, slandered, gossiped about, stolen from—*sinned* against. We are both perpetrator *and* victim, guilty *and* wounded.

One of the generational corrections that's come from millennials and Gen Z (with all sorts of *over*corrections, of course; that's how it inevitably works) is the recognition that *our wickedness is tied to our woundedness.* "Hurt people hurt people," as the saying goes, and it's true.

Starting in our earliest days, we accumulate a coterie of painful memories that we carry implicitly in our bodies, and tragically, against all our best intentions, we often pass them on to those closest to us. Cue the heart-wrenching stats on the number of abusers who were abused, cheaters who were cheated on, criticizers who were criticized, and so on.

A *key* part of our spiritual journeys to wholeness, especially for those who have been through traumatic life experiences, is the healing of memories, in both our minds and our bodies. The mending of souls ruptured by sin done *to* us.

Finally, there is . . .

#3 Sin done *around* us

Because of our hyper-individualistic culture, we often miss this last dimension, but Scripture's testimony is unequivocal: Our environment has warped us. Call it "secondary trauma," as psychologists do, or "the world" as Jesus did; it's like breathing secondhand smoke or toxic air—no one would hold you guilty in a court of law, but that doesn't make it any less lethal.

This is one of the best ways to make sense of the Christian doctrine of original sin. Here's Kallistos Ware:

> The doctrine of original sin means . . . that we are born into an environment where it is easy to do evil and hard to do good; easy to hurt others, and hard to heal their wounds; easy to arouse men's suspicions, and hard to win their trust. It means that we are each of us conditioned by the solidarity of the human race in its accumulated wrong-doing and wrong-thinking, and hence wrong-being. And to this accumulation of wrong we have ourselves added by our own deliberate acts of sin. The gulf grows wider and wider.[35]

This is so well said: We live in a world where it's "hard to do good."

—

Now, here's why I offer you this threefold rubric (it's not to depress you): Most people focus on dimension #1 of sin but not #2 and #3, and as a result, we don't realize just how desperate our situation is.

One reason for this is that Western Christians (Protestant and Catholic, but especially Protestant) have predominantly thought about sin through the guilt/innocence paradigm—what theologians call a "forensic" (that is, legal) view of sin. The basic idea is that God is a *morally serious* God; he is not only loving and compassionate but also holy and just. We are guilty before his law of justice, and our only hope is Christ's pardon. And the good news is that Christ is both "just and the justifier."[36]

This is a biblical view, but it's not *the* biblical view. It's just the one that has been emphasized in the West for the last few centuries. Many people don't realize there are all sorts of other paradigms (called "atonement theories") to understand sin in the library of Scripture:

- Guilt/Innocence

- Honor/Shame

- Power/Fear

- Clean/Defiled

- Belong/Lost

- Shalom/Chaos

- Hope/Despair[37]

Just to name a few. All of these are true, and *none* of them contradict or compete for primacy. The problem is not that Westerners view sin through the lens of guilt/innocence, but that they often view it *solely* from this one angle and, in doing so, miss the full picture. Until we come to see sin as far *more* than the breaking of judicial laws, we will likely remain stuck in whole-life dysfunction.

To that end, one paradigm that I find especially helpful for spiritual formation purposes is the idea of sin as a kind of disease of the soul and salvation as the healing of the whole person. As the Christian psychologist and expert on trauma Dan Allender put it, "We seldom see sin, at first sight, as what it truly is—ill and deforming."[38]

Jesus famously said, "It is not the healthy who need a doctor, but the sick. I have not come to call the righteous, but sinners to repentance."[39] In his analogy, sin was like a sickness and he was the doctor. Repentance wasn't just pleading for mercy before a judge; it was opening your wounding to a physician. Based on this line, ancient Christians called Jesus "the doctor of the soul."

Listen to Ignatius of Antioch, a first-century church father who was mentored by the apostle John. (This will give you insight into how early Christian leaders thought about salvation.) He said,

> But our Physician is the only true God . . . Jesus the Christ. . . . He became subject to corruption, that He might free our souls from death and corruption, and heal them, and might restore them to health, when they were diseased with ungodliness and wicked lusts.[40]

Is this how you think about sin? As a fatal disease?

Is this how you think about Jesus? As the physician of the soul?

Few people realize that the Greek word translated "saved" in the New Testament is *sōzō*—a word that is often translated "healed."[41] So, in the Gospels, when you read that Jesus "saved" someone and then read that he "healed" someone, *you're often reading the exact same word.* Jesus intentionally blurred the line between salvation and healing. Once, after healing a woman of a twelve-year chronic disease, Jesus said, "Daughter, your faith has *healed* you. Go in peace."[42] Some translations say "healed you," and others say "saved you." Why? Because salvation *is* a kind of healing.

Salvation is not *just* about getting back on the right side of God's mercy through judicial acquittal; it's about having your soul healed by God's loving touch. Ironically, the same sin that keeps us from relationship *with* God can be healed only *by* God. Yet again, we need to be saved.

And the beginning of our healing/salvation is what Christians call "confession." Confession is a core practice of the Way, and contrary to what many think, it's not at all about beating yourself up in public. It's about courageously naming your woundedness and wickedness in the presence of loving community as you journey together toward wholeness. It's about not only the confession of sin but also the confession of what is *true*—who you are, who *Christ* is, and who you truly are *in* Christ. It's about coming out of hiding into acceptance, leaving behind all shame.

And confession is *our* part in dealing with sin. God is the physician; we're the patient. All we can do is set our sin in his light. His job is to deal with our sin; *our job is to confess our secrets.* It's to live in a way that is open, true, and laid bare before God in community.

The best example of confession I can think of is, again, from AA. When people say "Hi, my name is _____, and I'm an alcoholic" to introduce themselves, *that's* confession, far more than saying sorry to God in our minds at church.

It's highly likely that any working model of spiritual formation will bear all sorts of resemblance to AA,[43] with its three elements of (1) radical self-awareness, honesty, and confession, (2) total surrender to God's power, and (3) a loving, tight-knit community to both love you and hold you accountable to becoming your true self. Take away any one of these tripart elements, and the proverbial stool will fall.

What I'm saying is this: The journey to healing *begins* with naming your illness. As the activist James Baldwin once said, "Not everything that is faced can be changed; but nothing can be changed until it is faced."[44]

The problem is: Human beings resist facing reality. The human capacity for self-deception is staggering. But when it comes to sin, ignorance is *not* bliss. It's a cancer metastasizing through our bloodstreams. The diagnosis is essential to the cure. Over a millennia and a half ago, Evagrius Ponticus said, "The beginning of salvation is to condemn oneself." He was just saying that until we name our sin and open our wound to God, we can't be saved from it.

This means we must begin by setting *all* that we are before God's loving eye. It is only when we are honest with God, others, and ourselves about all the ways we fall short of love that we enter into the transformational process of becoming more loving.

Put another way, *the more we hide, the less we heal*.

Problem #2: You've already been formed

But let's say I'm completely out to lunch; you have no cancer of the soul in need of healing—you are inherently good and whole and capable all by yourself. Again, we Christians don't buy this, but for the sake of argument, let's say your soul begins as a blank slate. (*Cough, cough . . .*)

If your goal is to become like Jesus, you still have a major problem: *You've already been formed.*

How we become *who* we become is a sacred mystery, taunting the brightest minds of both science and spirituality, so we must approach this question with a spirit of genuine humility. But there is a surprising level of agreement across traditions and disciplines.

We are formed by at least three basic forces.

#1 The stories we believe

We're story creatures. The screenwriter Bobette Buster argues that human beings are narrative animals. Our central nervous system is wired by God to search for meaning, to make what neurologists call "mental maps" of reality. In the same way that we have mental maps for how to get from our homes to work or the grocery store or our favorite coffee spot, we have mental maps for *all* of life—sex, relationships, money, work, God, etc. Stories about what the good life is and how to find it.

The stories we come to believe give shape to a thousand daily decisions, they give shape to what we do (or don't do) and who we become. As my friend Pete Hughes of King's Cross Church in London likes to say, "The story you live in is the story you live out."[45]

Let's take money, for example: If you believe the popular Western story that more money equals more happiness, that the good life is about accomplishment and accumulation, it will *form* you into a certain kind of person—driven, greedy, envious, discontent, distracted from God, never satisfied, and maybe even dishonest and cruel.

On the other hand, if you believe Jesus' view of money, that all the good things in our lives are God's gifts, but that wealth makes it *harder,* not easier, for most of us to enter the kingdom; that freedom from our latent desire for more is found through giving, not getting; and that following his Way of simplicity, generosity, and hospitality will help us live "freely and lightly . . ."[46] If you believe *that* story, it will form you too—into a very different, more Jesus-y kind of person.

Pick your stories carefully.

They will determine who you become.

Next, we are formed by . . .

#2 Our habits

All sorts of work has been done over the last few decades to highlight what the journalist Charles Duhigg called the "power of habit."[47] Synopsis: We are little more than the cumulative effect of our regular habits. What we repeatedly do, we become.

The things we do, do something *to* us; they get into the core of our being and shape our loves and longings.

We think we're just watching Hulu or sipping *another* glass of wine or buying a new shirt, but more is going on below the surface: We're doing something to our hearts. We're turning the fulcrum of our inner persons in a particular direction.

Again, by itself, this is morally neutral; it could be good or bad.

My point is, it *is.*

What we do, we become.

Finally . . .

#3 Our relationships

You don't need a PhD in clinical psychology to realize that we become like the people we spend time with. The odds are that you dress, vote, think, spend money, and *live* like your friends.

All of us do. We become *like* the people we love and do life with.

Nowhere is this truer than in our families of origin. As the saying goes, "Jesus may be in your heart, but grandpa is in your bones!"[48] But it's also true of our ethnicity, nationality, city, alma mater, workplace, digital echo chamber, and more.

As disciples of Jesus, we must carefully discern the ways that we've been formed (or malformed)—not by the kingdom but by our last names, our family lines, our political tribes, or our zip codes.

Here's the simple point I've been driving to for pages: *You are right now, currently, as we speak, being formed* by a complex web of ideas, cultural narratives, reoccurring thoughts, habits, daily rhythms, spending patterns, relationships, family ties, activities, environments, and much more. *Just by waking up and going about your life.*

We don't get the luxury of a blank slate; there are forces—within and without—with a vested interest in us *not* becoming like Jesus.

Therefore: *All Christian formation is counter-formation.*

In Romans 12v2, Paul writes,

> Do not conform to the pattern of this world, but be transformed.

Notice, there are two options: "conform" or "be transformed." To go full Bible nerd on you, both verbs are in the present passive imperative. Translation: It's a command to keep on doing something that's *already* happening. You're *already* being *conformed* or *transformed*.

There is no option C.

Paul is writing to disciples of Jesus in the city of Rome, a formation machine that makes L.A. pale in comparison. The express goal of the imperial propaganda arm was to take citizens from across a wide array of colonized cultures and make them more *Roman;* Paul's goal was to take Romans and make them more *Christ-ian.*

But notice also that the default setting is conformation, *not* transformation. Meaning, if we don't take our discipleship to Jesus seriously, the odds are very high that we will become *less* like Jesus over time and *more* like "Rome" (or L.A., or London, or Lagos, and so on).

The novelist Flannery O'Connor once advised, "Push as hard as the age that pushes against you."[49] We have to push back on the forces that seek to deform us, to keep us from reaching our potential in Jesus.

This will likely start with, again, a kind of formation audit—an honest look at all the current forces in our lives that are deforming us into the image of the world, the flesh, and the devil *and* their intentional replacement with stories, habits, and relationships to index us toward formation into the image of Jesus. It will require us to embrace that *all* of life is spiritual formation. Each moment of each day is like a liturgy, a sacred ritual designed to shape our hearts. As Tish Harrison Warren wrote in her book *Liturgy of the Ordinary* (a must-read for all young parents),

> Examining my daily liturgy *as a liturgy*—as something that both revealed and shaped what I love and worship—allowed me to realize that my daily practices were malforming me, making me less alive, less human, less able to give and receive love throughout my day.[50]

The alternative is to practice the Way, to take up a whole constellation of life choices that's different from the majority culture around us—to make choices that aim our love and longing at union with God and our formation into his likeness.

We can push back.

We can partner with Jesus to become *like* Jesus, a human being who is, as the ancient sage Irenaeus put it, "fully alive."

Of course, this raises an essential question: *How?*

A working theory of change

Disclaimer: What you are about to read is not capital *T* True.

But it may be helpful.

What follows is my best attempt at a synthesis of Scripture, psychology, neurobiology, the best of the social sciences, literature, poetry, and more.

I call it a working theory because it's a *theory,* not cold, hard fact, but also because it *works.* I've spent years living into this paradigm as both a pastor and apprentice of Jesus, and while there is no magic formula for the soul, I find this to be a reliable pathway to transformation.

To adequately cover the following theory of change will require another book, but let me give you a thirty-thousand-foot overview. Here's my best take at counter-formation.

Intentional Spiritual Formation

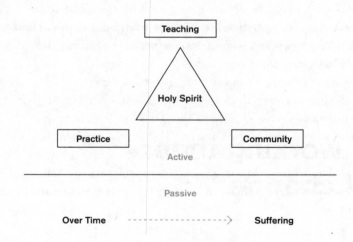

Counter to the stories we believe is . . .

#1 Teaching

Another word to use here is *truth*. Jesus came as a rabbi, a teacher, a truth teller. Why? Because the role of truth is central to our spiritual formation.

As I wrote in *Live No Lies,* one thing that separates humans from the animals is our capacity for imagination. We have the ability to hold unreality in our minds—to imagine what does not yet exist—and then bring it into reality through our bodies. This is what enables all human creativity, from writing a novel to flying to Mars to cooking enchiladas. Tragically, this capacity is also our Achilles' heel, because, not only can we hold unreality in our minds, but also we can come to *believe* that unreality. We can put our trust in lies and then, through our bodies, live as if those lies were true.

This is why when the devil comes to Eve in the Garden, he doesn't come with a stick but with an idea. Because ideas and the idea systems of fallen society are the primary trade of the evil one. They cause us to believe lies.

But the *best* teaching does more than just inform us—it gets into our heads with a vision of the good life. It undermines the untrue stories we believe; it says, "This is *true,* and this is a *lie.*" It shifts our trust. It rewires our mental maps to reality, making it possible for us to live in alignment with reality in such a way that we flourish and thrive according to God's wisdom and good intentions.

Of course, nowhere is this more true than in the teaching we receive about God. As Tozer famously said, "What comes into our minds when we think about God is the most important thing about us,"[51] because we become like our mental picture of God.

For this reason, spiritual formation in the Way of Jesus *begins* with the healing of our false images of God. If a person's vision of God is distorted—if they view him as harsh, demeaning, or chronically angry . . . or as liberal, laissez-faire, and simply there to champion their sexual pleasure—the more religious they become, *the worse they become*. Because we become *like* who we believe God *is*.

So, to counter the daily barrage of straight-up lies we receive from the world around us, as apprentices of Jesus we must, like good students, prioritize exposure to teaching and truth. There are all sorts of ways to do this:

- Reading Scripture

- Memorizing Scripture

- Studying the Bible

- Listening to sermons

- Listening to podcasts

- Reading books

- Meditating

Just to name a few.

Paul called this "the renewing of your mind," and it is the linch-pin of our formation.

But getting the right ideas in our mindstream is just the beginning. Remember that information alone is not enough to change.

Next, counter to our habits are . . .

#2 The practices

In the biographer Matthew's telling of the Jesus story, we find the single most important collection of Jesus' teachings all grouped into one place. We call it "the Sermon on the Mount," and it is a treasure beyond value. Tragically, there is a *long*-standing tradition in the church of finding creative ways to explain it away. Many theologians have argued that it's unrealistic to live this way, that it simply cannot be done. But on a close reading, you realize: While Jesus does set a high bar, he's incredibly in tune with the limits of our humanity. Jesus assumes that we will lust and want to get a divorce and call people names and love money and worry about our future. But what's easy to miss is that Jesus also assumes that living his Way is going to take practice.

One of the *first* things Jesus says, right before his opening command, is:

> Whoever *practices* and teaches these commands will be called great in the kingdom of heaven.[52]

And the literal *last* thing Jesus says is an echo:

> Therefore everyone who hears these words of mine and puts them into *practice* . . . [53]

Jesus begins *and* ends the Sermon on the Mount with a call to practice.

And yet, very few of us think of following Jesus as a *practice*.

Back to Richard Foster: After decades of teaching on spiritual formation all over North America, he concluded that most people think they will grow to be more like Jesus through *trying* hard rather than *training* hard, when the exact opposite is true.

Let me offer you an analogy: Let's say you're out of shape, overweight, and asthmatic, but you decide you want to run a marathon.

How do you do it?

Do you buy a pair of Nikes, walk outside, and just try *very* hard to run 26.2 miles? Of course not; that's a fool's errand. What would happen? You would make it a few miles and then collapse on the side of the road leaking lung fluid. Why? Because you are not currently the kind of person for whom it is possible to run 26.2 miles.

It's not impossible to run a marathon, but it is for you, *now,* as you are.

So, how do you do it?

Simple: You train. You lace up your shoes, walk outside, and run *one* mile. Every day (minus the Sabbath). The following week, you run *two* miles. The next week, three. If you've ever run a marathon, you know that you basically add a mile each week to your "long run." Three miles becomes five becomes ten becomes twenty.

And what happens?

Over a long period of time—through *training*—you *change;* you become the kind of person for whom running 26.2 miles is hard (as it will *always* be hard), but it is no longer impossible. It is now within your capacity as a person. And then come those sweet feelings after all your training: health, energy, capacity, and joy.

We run a marathon one mile at a time.

The problem is, *very few* of us approach our formation this way—by training.

Now, this analogy breaks down, as all do. For the record, I'm not saying we can habit stack our way into Christlikeness through Pelagian self-effort alone. (Good luck.) Remember what I said about grace. We need a power beyond us to change. (More on that coming soon . . .)

I'm saying we need to *practice* the Way of Jesus, not just go out and try to do it. For all the pro-grace, anti-works talk in the church, many people still attempt to live out Jesus' teachings based on biblical knowledge and willpower alone. We hear clichés like "Rely on God" or "You can't do it in your own strength." All true, but rarely do we learn *how* to rely on grace and draw on God's energies when we most need them.

So, let's sharpen the focus on this idea of practice and give it more of an edge: What I mean by *practice* is more accurately the *practices* of Jesus, also known as the spiritual disciplines. These are essentially activities we undertake as disciples of Jesus that re-habituate the automatic responses of sin in our bodies and replace them with the intuitions of the Spirit. They are attempts to copy the example of Jesus' lifestyle, in the hope of experiencing his *life*—the life we crave in the marrow of our bones.

So, for example, let's say you want to obey Jesus' teaching in the Sermon on the Mount to "not worry." You want to become a non-anxious presence in the world. How do you do it? Do you listen to a good sermon on Matthew 6 and then just go out and . . . not worry?

How's that working for you?

I'm guessing it's *not*.

For most of us, being told to live without anxiety is like being told to run a marathon. We can't do it. Not *yet*. So, how do we live without worry? Well, we have to *become the kinds of people who have learned to trust in God so deeply that we are free of fear*. To do *that*, we must train (or retrain) our minds and bodies. So, yes, we listen to a good sermon on Matthew 6, *and* . . . we practice Sabbath; we set aside an entire day to practice trusting God. *And* . . . we spend time in the secret place, where we lay all our fears at God's feet. *And* . . . we live in community, where others encourage us to trust in God. *And* . . . we practice generosity to free our hearts from empty loves. *And* . . . etc., etc. And over *a long period of time,* our anxiety is gradually replaced by a peace and unshakable trust in God.

Training, not trying.

Practice.

#3 Community

You can't follow Jesus alone.

Not "shouldn't"; *can't.*

It's not even an option. Jesus didn't have a disciple; he had *disciples,* plural. He called people to apprentice under him in community.

Community is like the incubator for our spiritual formation. As Dr. Joseph Hellerman put it, "Long-term interpersonal relationships are the crucible of genuine progress in the Christian life. People who stay also grow. People who leave do not grow."[54]

Salvation itself is a communal experience. One of the primary pictures of salvation in the New Testament is that of adoption. Through Jesus' atoning work, we have been adopted into the family of God. As an adoptive father, that picture is especially poignant to me. When T and I adopted our daughter, Sunday, she instantly became my daughter and Jude and Moses's sister. The kids get along quite well (mostly), but even if they didn't, she doesn't have a choice—for her to be a Comer is to be both a daughter *and* a sister. The same is true of our salvation: We become both sons and daughters of God the Father and brothers and sisters to one another. And this is good news, even when it's so very hard, because at the core of what's broken in the human condition is ruined relationships—with both God *and* people. Love has been shattered by the fall. Hurt, betrayal, and loneliness mar the human soul. Jesus has saved, is saving, and will save us from this ruin by forming (through his apprenticeship program) a glorious new family of love.

As we wait for this unveiling, it's vital that we participate in the "now and not yet" iteration of Jesus' family, the church, which is both beautiful and deeply flawed.

Serious Christians often argue about the best *form* of community: Is it a megachurch or a house church? Or we debate the finer points of church tradition: liturgical versus Pentecostal versus sermon-centric, etc. But the older I get, the less concerned I am with form and tradition; they each have pros and cons. The key is to be aware of them, and do the best you can. Now I'm much more concerned with the *culture* of a church. Whether there are thousands of people around a stage or ten or fifteen around a table, whether they are worshipping to modern rock ballads or quietly reading ancient prayers, I'm interested in *this* question: Does the community call people *up* to a higher level of apprenticeship? Or does it devolve to the lowest common denominator of maturity (or immaturity)?

Of course, talking about church in the abstract is dangerous. As Bonhoeffer said, "Those who love their dream of a Christian community more than they love the Christian community itself become destroyers of that Christian community even though their personal intentions may be ever so honest, earnest, and sacrificial."[55] He called this the "wish dream" of an ideal church. No *actual* church can *ever* live up to the wish dream of an *ideal* church. So, people either give up on church entirely or settle into cynicism: "The church is a whore, but she's my mother," as the terrible saying goes.

We must embrace *this* church, *this* pastor, *these* people. We must forgive *these* shortcomings and celebrate *these* strengths. Community is always a nonabstract journey into facing *reality.*

Honestly, I can tell you from over a decade of living in very close community, it's *not* easy, but it's worth it. We can all tell stories of how deep the pain cuts when it goes horribly wrong, but when it goes right . . .

It's a glimpse of eternity in time.

Next, is . . .

#4 The Holy Spirit

Now we're back to the practice of the presence of God.

He is the ultimate source of our transformation.

This is where the marathon analogy falls woefully short. The practices don't just strengthen our willpower muscle (as with running); they open us to a power from *beyond* us—the power to change.

Yes, we have a part to play in our formation, alongside God. But this partnership is *not* fifty-fifty. I don't have an accurate breakdown, but let's just say, he does all the heavy lifting. It is his power—his alone—that can change, heal, fix, and renew the most damaged corners of our souls.

Christlikeness in our inner being is not the result of the right application of spiritual disciplines, finding a "good church," or mastering the right technique of living—it is always a gift of sheer grace. You will never work harder for anything in your life than Christlike character, and nothing else will ever feel like such an unearned gift. This is a paradox you simply have to experience for yourself.

When we arrive at the end of our long journey and look back at how far we've come, we will exclaim with all the saints, "Salvation"—rightly understood as the healing of our whole person—"belongs to our God."[56]

Finally, this happens . . .

#5 Over time

We do not become like Jesus overnight, but through a "long obedience in the same direction."[57] This is a tough sell in our culture of instant gratification, but there's no Blinkist for the soul. It takes *time*.

Of course, "time" here is double entendre: (1) Our formation will take a *long* time—a *lifetime*. But (2) it will also take *a lot* of time. And like any relationship, the more time you put in, the more you will get out.

So, how long someone has been following Jesus is a major factor in their maturity level, but so is *how much time* they give *to* Jesus in their daily life.

"I'm too busy" is the number one excuse/obstacle most people face in formation. But the hard truth is, most of us *waste* copious amounts of time. Cue all the stats: The average millennial is on their phone nearly four hours a day;[58] most adults ages thirty-five to forty-four watch two to three hours of TV a *day*. Combined, that's almost a full-time job. Think of what we could do with even a tithe of that time.

Whatever you decide, the key to becoming a saint is to keep walking behind Jesus for the long haul. As the saying goes, "A black belt is just a white belt who never quit." A saint is just an ordinary apprentice who stayed at it with Jesus.

Last . . .

#6 Through suffering

One final thought *none* of us want to hear: The most difficult moments in our lives—the ones we fear and avoid at all costs— are our crucibles. They have the most potential to forge our souls into the shape of Jesus.

All the New Testament writers attest to this sacred mystery.

James tells us to "consider it pure *joy*" when we "face trials of many kinds," because they generate "perseverance" in us and, in time, maturity.[59] Paul writes that perseverance will in turn create "character; and character, hope."[60] Peter urges us to "greatly rejoice"[61] in our trials because they are like a refining fire, burning off the dross to reveal the gold.

Can you see it?

It's the very things we run from, avoid at all costs, dread, medicate, and deny that hold the secret to our liberation. These unhappy times of great emotional pain, in a beautifully redemptive turn, have the potential—if we open to God in them—to transform us into grounded, deeply joyful people. Suffering is sadness leaving the body.

Where does your soul hurt? A pain of the heart that can be expressed only in a groan . . .

This could be your moment of liberation.

Only one thing is required: Open your pain to God . . .

So, to circle back to our question: Can we really become like Jesus? Is transformation possible?

Yes, it is.

But it's not inevitable.

It will take an intentional plan for counter-formation, what I'll define later in the book as a Rule of Life.

But you *can* change, you can grow, you can get free, and you can find healing.

Or as Jesus would say, you can be saved.

Terrible, wonderful news: You are not in control

But let me make one last thing perfectly clear: You are not in control of your spiritual formation. This is one of the *hardest* lessons for followers of Jesus today: We can't control our spiritual journeys, most of the circumstances of our lives, and certainly not God.

Ours is the digital age. Indeed, one interpretation of the sociopolitical chaos of the last few years in America and beyond is that it's not about politics at all; it's about the social disruption caused by the shift from an industrial to a digital world.[62] We're living through a key inflection point in human history, and we're feeling the vertigo of an entire world turned upside down in just a few decades.

I grew up in Silicon Valley, and I'm well aware of the power of tech for good. But for all the genuine value it's added to the world, digital technology has had at least three disastrous effects on our generation's formation.

It's formed us to expect life to be

1. Easy

2. Fast

3. And controllable

After all, we can just slide our thumb and dinner will magically appear at our door twenty minutes later. . . .

As a result, we are conditioned to expect quick, fast results with minimal effort, all at our beck and call. We often carry this mindset over into our formation—we assume we just need to find the right technique or life hack to solve the problem of the soul.

But in reality, formation into the image of Jesus is

1. Hard

2. Slow

3. And we are *not* in control

There's no killer app, no quick fix, no shortcut. The formation of the human soul is more like growing a vineyard than ordering takeout.

The danger with laying out a working theory of change is that we can be deluded into thinking, *If I just master the right spiritual technique, I can form myself into the perfect person.* Trust me, life will unmask that illusion for the cruel joke it is.

The French philosopher Jacques Ellul once compared the Western obsession with "technique" to magic in the Middle Ages. It's a modern form of superstition that's *all* about trying to control what we cannot possibly control.[63]

This is where, for those of us with more control-oriented personalities, there's a latent danger in taking our spiritual formation seriously. The practices of spiritual formation can be perverted into yet another attempt at control—rather than a medium through which we release the illusion of control back to God, and open ourselves to grace.

While this truth will likely grate against our preferences, it's *great* news. Truly. We can't self-save, *and we don't have to.* We have been saved, are *being* saved, and will be saved by Jesus and him alone. He's the savior, not us. He's the good shepherd; our role is just to follow. And to *keep* following through all the highs and lows along the Way.

It may take a long time—years, decades even—to become who we know we were meant to be. We may not see the payoff until we're in our sixties, or later. Like the transformation of a caterpillar into a butterfly, it may take a long time of darkness and struggle until we emerge beautified, and it may not be until the very end of our journeys this side of eternity. *But it will be* more *than worth it.* As Jesus put it, we will be like the mother who, after the excruciating pain of labor, "forgets the anguish because of her joy that a child is born into the world."[64]

Something approaching Christlikeness *is* possible in this life. It really is. We can be healed, we can be set free of broken patterns that stretch back generations, we can be transformed into people who are genuinely pervaded by love and joy and peace. Our souls can throb with the bliss of union with God. Our bodies can become temples; our neighborhoods, holy ground; our days, eternity in time; our moments, miracles.

All in good time . . .

For now, the master's call is simple: Follow me.

Practicing the Way—

Goal #3:
Do as he did

—

"Go and make apprentices of all kinds of people."[1] So read Jesus' closing words to his apprentices.

This is *exactly* what you would expect a rabbi to say to his students at the end of their training. Remember, a rabbi's goal wasn't just to teach, but also to raise up disciples after himself to *carry on* his teaching and way of life. To this day, upon their ordination rabbis are commissioned to "raise up many disciples," in a liturgy dating back to the time of Jesus.[2]

When Jesus called Simon and Andrew to "follow me, and I will make you become fishers of men,"[3] that wasn't a cheesy preacher pun, nor was it a call to snatch people from the precipice of hell. In the first century, "fishers of men" was an honorific for great rabbis,[4] because the best teachers had the power to capture the minds and imaginations of their listeners.

Jesus was saying, "Apprentice under me, and *I will teach you to do what I do.*"

In Acts 1, the historian Luke wrote, "In my former book [*The Gospel of Luke*], . . . I wrote about all that Jesus began to do and to teach."

Note the verb: *began.*

The implication is, *this* book is about what Jesus' disciples *continue* to do and to teach.

And that's exactly how *Acts* reads, as a continuation of Jesus' work. *All* the things you read about Jesus doing in *Luke*—healing the sick, casting out demons, preaching the gospel—you read about his *apprentices* doing in *Acts*.

Again, this is exactly what you would expect to happen to a *talmid* upon their completion of an apprenticeship program: to do as their rabbi did.

Learning theorists frame apprenticeship as a four-stage training process:

1. I do; you watch.

2. I do; you help.

3. You do; I help.

4. You do; I watch.[5]

You can map this exact process onto Jesus' training of his apprentices. At first they just followed him around and watched; over time they began to help Jesus; then they began to do Jesus' work, a little at a time, receiving a lot of feedback as they took their first faltering steps; and by the end, they were sent out in Jesus' name and power to continue what he started.

All this is leading us to goal #3: Do as he did. The final goal of an apprentice is to carry on the work of the master. At the end of the day, that's what apprenticeship is ultimately *for*.

In our church, we have a plumber's apprentice who is in the middle of a four-year training program. Upon graduation, his goal isn't just to have read a lot of books about plumbing or to have fixed the occasional leaky faucet in his bathroom; *it's to become a plumber.*

We also have a number of medical students in our community. That's an even longer training program—twelve-plus years. Chatting with these students, I can assure you that their end goal isn't just to watch *Grey's Anatomy* and know all the lingo; it's to become doctors and *practice* medicine.

Now, track with me, as this is a very simple idea that's lost on so many Christians: If you are an apprentice of Jesus, *your end goal is to grow and mature into the kind of person who can say and do all the things Jesus said and did.*

Children often get this intuitively; they read the story of the good Samaritan, and their first impulse is to stop every time you drive by somebody with a flat tire. After all, Jesus ended that story by saying, "Go and do likewise."[6] Or they hear the stories of Jesus healing the sick, and the next time their friend from preschool has a cold, they hug them and pray for them to get better. But something happens to us over time where we are socially conditioned to dampen that impulse.

What if that impulse is the Spirit?

What if that inner prompt of the heart is the Spirit working in us to go and do the kinds of things Jesus did?

Or to be more precise, the kinds of things Jesus would do if he were *us*? Willard defined a disciple as someone whose ultimate goal is to live their life the way Jesus would live if he were me.

Remember WWJD? What would Jesus do? It's a fine question, but a much *better* question is WWJDIHWM? What would Jesus do *if he were me*?

Why is it better? Because the odds are that you're not a first-century, celibate Jewish rabbi; you're a twenty-first-century mom, freshman at uni, VP of a startup, freelance graphic designer, or my secret dream—a luchador.

It's a bit hard to ask WWJD if your current work is raising a two-year-old or teaching kindergarten or writing software or designing the HVAC system for a new building downtown—much less doing any of the latter *while* raising your two-year-old. Instead, ask this: How would Jesus live if he had my gender, place, personality profile, age, life stage, job, resources, and address? How would he show up to the world? How would he handle
_____?

For the apprentice of Jesus, *that* is the question all of life becomes an attempt to answer.

As Jesus' apprentice John put it in the New Testament, "This is how we know we are in him: Whoever claims to live in him must *live as Jesus did*."[7]

Now, right about here is where I lose you.

Anytime I talk about Jesus as the example of how to live, people think, *Yeah, sure, but he was God. I'm just . . . well,* me. *It's not like I can go out and heal the sick and do miracles and such . . .*

Right?

Jesus the prototype

The New Testament writers call Jesus the "the firstfruits"—this is an agrarian analogy from Jesus' first-century world. The first-fruits were the first buds of the fall harvest, a sign of what's about to erupt en masse. Jesus is that first sign of what's coming for *all* his followers; some scholars translate the Greek as "proto-type,"[8] the first of a whole new kind of human. Translation: Who Jesus *was* in his time on earth is an advanced version of who we have the potential to *become* in him. Jesus is the template for you and me to pour our lives into.

Unfortunately, most Western Christians read the stories about Jesus, especially the miracle stories, not as a template for how to live but as "proof that Jesus was God." This goes back hundreds of years to the Enlightenment, when Western elites began to say, "We believe Jesus was a great teacher, sure, but nothing more." (This then let *them* decide which of his teachings to follow or ignore and, as a result, let *them* run the world as they saw fit[9]—a pattern that continues to this day.)

The counterargument from serious Christians was "But look at the miracle stories! A mere *man* can't heal the sick and cast out demons, much less turn water into wine or walk on water!"[10] This is a *well-intentioned* argument, but there's a fatal flaw in its logic, as well as a completely unintended but disastrous conse-quence.

First, the fatal flaw: Yes, Jesus did miracles, *but so did his disciples and the Hebrew prophets before them.* Read *The Book of Acts*—the apostles healed the sick, cast out demons, and even raised the dead! Yet no one claims that's "proof they were God."

You see the problem?

And the tragic consequence of this faulty logic is this: If we assume that Jesus did the stuff he did "because he was God," we will then assume we *can't* do the stuff he did because we're *not* God, clearly. $1 + 1 = 2$.

But this raises a provocative theological question: Where did Jesus get his power? Ordinary people do not walk around raising the dead.

The short answer: from the Holy Spirit.

Luke's gospel is clearest on this note: "Jesus returned to Galilee in the power of the *Spirit*," where, on the Sabbath, he read from the scroll of Isaiah:

> The *Spirit* of the Lord is on me,
>   because he has anointed me
>   to proclaim good news to the poor.
> He has sent me to proclaim freedom for the prisoners
>   and recovery of sight for the blind,
> to set the oppressed free,
>   to proclaim the year of the Lord's favor.[11]

Interpretation: Jesus did what he did by drawing on his connection to the capacities of God.

My point is: Jesus did miracles not by flexing his God muscles like Thor but by living in reliance on the Spirit's power.

agree?

In Jesus' incarnation, we see what the real, true God is like. Not the God who is a figment of our imaginations or fears but the God who is reality. It's not just that "Jesus is God" but more like "God is Jesus." Or "God is Christlike and in him is no un-Christlikeness at all," as the Anglican Archbishop Michael Ramsey once said.[12] But listen carefully: In Jesus' incarnation we *also* see *what a real, true human being is like.* We see what God had in mind from the beginning—what human beings have the potential to become if reunited with God.

So, when you read the miracle stories, don't just think, *Oh, well, Jesus was God.* Yes, he was. But *also* think, *Wow, this is what a real, true human being, walking in the power of the Spirit, is capable of.*

Right before his death, Jesus said this:

> Whoever believes in me will do the works I have been doing . . .

What had Jesus been doing? Healing the sick, delivering the demonized, doing miracles, and so on.

> They will do even greater things than these, because I am going to the Father. [13]

Greater?

Than *miracles?*

New Testament scholars debate what exactly Jesus means here by "greater things than these."[14] But on this they align: Whatever he means by "greater things," *he doesn't mean* lesser *things.*

Now, I'm not saying you need to rush down to your local morgue and get your holy roller on. I'm just saying that the same power that was on Jesus, and then on Peter, Paul, and the earliest apostles, *is now on you and me*—or at least *is available* to you and me as we, like Jesus, surrender to the Father and open ourselves to the Spirit's promptings.

This is the only possible way we can "do what Jesus would do if he were me." If *Jesus* did his work in the power of the Spirit, *how much more* do we need the Spirit to carry on that same work?

Thankfully, there's good news: Jesus did not leave us dependent on our natural abilities, talents, and energies (or lack thereof). He gave us his Spirit to empower us with *his* capacities. To do *his* work by *his* power, not our work by our own very limited resources.

Jesus is looking for disciples he can trust with his power.

Do you want to become one?

The kind of person who can steward power with grace?

To "go into all the world" and do as he did/would do if he were you?

If you've made it this far in the book, you're likely thinking, *Yes.* Good.

Of course, this raises a very interesting question: What exactly did Jesus do?

The spiritual writer Henri Nouwen once said Jesus' life moved along a continuum from solitude to community to ministry.[15]

What was Jesus' "ministry"?

What did he *do* to usher in God's kingdom?

There's no official list of what Jesus did (just as there's no official list of the practices), but I find it helpful to categorize Jesus' ministry into three basic rhythms:

1. Making space for the gospel

2. Preaching the gospel

3. Demonstrating the gospel

Rhythm #1: Making space for the gospel (i.e., hospitality)

It's no secret that our increasingly post-Christian culture is no longer warm or even neutral to the gospel—it's *hostile* to it. Many people perceive "Christianity" as part of the problem, not the solution.[16] Most secular people have zero interest in hearing the gospel, preferring to look for salvation in other sources.

But we've been here before. Many people in Jesus' day were just as hostile to the gospel—so hostile they eventually killed him.

How do we make space for God in such an emotionally loaded atmosphere?

The same way he did: by eating and drinking.

Luke 19 recounts a heartwarming story about Jesus inviting himself over to Zacchaeus's home for dinner. Zacchaeus was a tax collector who made a (very lucrative) living by defrauding his fellow Jews on behalf of the Roman Empire. Imagine a Nazi informer in Poland during the Holocaust. You can imagine how he would have been *hated*. Yet here was Jesus, at his table—less guest and more *host*. As a result, Zacchaeus became an apprentice of Jesus.

Yet "all the people saw this and began to mutter, 'He has gone to be the guest of a sinner.'"[17]

We find the story heartwarming, but they found it offensive. Why? Because meals are what the anthropologist Mary Douglas called "boundary markers."[18] Meals bring people together, but they also keep people apart. Think of the pre–civil rights restaurants with signs on the door saying WHITES ONLY, or, in the UK, NO IRISH, NO BLACKS, NO DOGS. Even today, think of how restaurants are often stratified by class. Even in the no-brow places we tend to love,[19] most of us eat with friends or family, people who are *like us*.

This is true of all cultures, but it was *especially* true of first-century Jewish culture. They called it "table fellowship"; to eat with someone was a sign of welcome, not just into one's home, but also into good standing with the community and even with God himself.

Hence, no self-respecting rabbi would ever be caught *dead* at the table of someone like Zacchaeus. It would be the end of his career.

One theologian wrote, "Jesus got himself crucified by the way he ate."[20] He ate with all the wrong people: turncoats like Zacchaeus, prostitutes, Gentiles, the unclean. Danger, danger. He was accused of being "a glutton and a drunkard, a friend of tax collectors and sinners."[21]

That was *not* a compliment.

You see, for Rabbi Jesus, meals were not a "boundary marker" but a sign of God's great welcome into the kingdom; not a way to keep people *out,* but to invite people *in.*

In *The Gospel of Luke* alone, there are over *fifty* references to food. Lukan scholar Robert Karris wrote, "In Luke's Gospel Jesus is either going to a meal, at a meal, or coming from a meal."[22]

I *like* this Jesus.

I think I will apprentice under him in all things . . .

The UK pastor Tim Chester wrote a great little book called *A Meal with Jesus,* where he pointed out there's an iconic verbal formula that's used two times in Luke: "The Son of Man came . . ."[23]

First, Luke wrote, "The Son of Man came to seek and to save the lost."[24]

That was *what* Jesus did—his *mission*.

Then he wrote, "The Son of Man came eating and drinking."[25]

That was *how* Jesus did it—his *method*.[26]

Jesus lived in a culture where a lot of people were hostile toward him. How did he invite them into his kingdom?

One meal at a time . . .

This practice of eating and drinking with people far from God is what the New Testament writers call "hospitality." The word is *philoxenia* in Greek, and it's a compound word: *philo* means "love," and *xenos* means "stranger, foreigner, or guest."[27] Meaning: Hospitality is the *opposite* of xenophobia. It's the *love* of the stranger, not the hate or fear of the "other." It's the act of welcoming the outsider *in* and, in doing so, turning guests into neighbors and neighbors into family in God.

We can't force a person to become a disciple of Jesus, nor would we want to. But we can offer them a space where such a change can occur, even if slowly over time. We can actively seek out the lonely, the newcomer, the uncool, the poor, the immigrant or refugee—those with no family or no home—and welcome them *in* to a community of love.

As Henri Nouwen so beautifully said,

In our world full of strangers, estranged from their own past, culture and country, from their neighbors, friends and family, from their deepest self and their God, we witness a painful search for a hospitable place where life can be lived without fear and where community can be found. . . . It is possible for men and women and obligatory for Christians to offer an open and hospitable space where strangers can cast off their strangeness and become our fellow human beings.[28]

You see, hospitality is both a rhythm we calendar into our Rule of Life, *and* it's a way of being in the world, a heart posture toward others. Nouwen called it "a fundamental attitude toward our fellow human being, which can be expressed in a great variety of ways."[29] When we offer hospitality, we get to embody the heart posture of the Trinity's inner life—welcome, invitation, warm affection, generosity, provision, safety, community, comfort, the meeting of needs, delight, and sheer joy. And "when we act like God, we get to feel like God,"[30] to share his joy.

The writer Rosaria Butterfield called this act "radically ordinary hospitality":

Radically ordinary hospitality—those who live it see strangers as neighbors and neighbors as family of God. They recoil at reducing a person to a category or a label. They see God's image reflected in the eyes of every human being on earth. . . .

Those who live out radically ordinary hospitality see their homes not as theirs at all but as God's gift to use for the furtherance of his kingdom. They open doors; they seek out the underprivileged. They know that the gospel comes with a house key.[31]

This was Jesus' way.

It is still the best way.

There's no better place to get to know someone than over a meal, no better place to dialogue and even disagree in love. Because of that, there's no better place to preach the gospel (the next rhythm) than around a table, with bread and wine. I'm no skilled evangelist; the next rhythm is a weakness in my discipleship, not a strength. But I can tell you this: After living in one of the most secular cities in the world, *all* of the best conversations I've *ever* had with people far from God have been around my table. All of them.

The *beauty* of Jesus' method is this:

1. It is something you're *already* doing. You already eat meals. All you have to do is repurpose a few of them to offer God's great welcome.

2. *Anyone* can do this. You don't need a seminary degree or expertise in apologetics; you don't need a formal dining room or a *Kinfolk*-worthy backyard with cool hanging lights. You just need a table. *And it doesn't even have to be yours.*

Rhythm #2: Preaching the gospel

A few days ago my teenage son came home distraught. "What happened?" I asked. Deep sigh. He had just been walking downtown with a friend and came across a group of Christians preaching "the gospel" on the street corner. It was textbook: They all had signs on poles—a bizarre mix of "Jesus loves you" and dire warnings about the fires of hell. Naturally, there was a bullhorn, and tracts were passed out. The friend he was walking with isn't a follower of Jesus, and Jude felt the group's "evangelism" would do nothing but push his friend *away* from God, not draw him in.

Like Jude, many of us cringe just *hearing* stories like this. These old methods feel tone-deaf and out of touch *at best,* if not manipulative and cruel. They rarely result in people discovering life through apprenticeship to Jesus.

So, when I say that rhythm #2 is "preaching the gospel," I have a minor allergic reaction—*not* because I don't love the gospel and care about the people Jesus called "lost," but because of all the cringeworthy examples that come to mind. I have no desire to be associated with *that* kind of preaching the gospel.

And yet: Even when I hear someone tell the good news of Jesus in a thoughtful, loving, culturally attuned way, I *still* feel a little bit anxious. And I'm not alone . . .

In our generation, the primary problem with evangelism *isn't* that we're doing it with bullhorns and low-grade bigotry; *it's that we're not doing it at all.*

In a recent poll by the Barna Group, 96 percent of millennial Christians said, "Part of my faith means being a witness about Jesus," and 94 percent said, "The best thing that could ever happen to someone is for them to come to know Jesus." But a full *47 percent*—nearly half—*also* said, "It is wrong to share one's personal beliefs with someone of a different faith in hopes that they will one day share the same faith."[32]

That is a jarring inconsistency, but it's not surprising given our times. We live in a pluralistic, postmodern culture where any form of Christian "proselytizing" is offensive to our modern sensibilities. We're socially conditioned from a young age to keep our mouths shut about Jesus; "faith is a private, not public, matter," we're told. "Who are *you* to tell *me* what is true?" is the sentiment. Because any form of truth claims, no matter how graciously presented, pass implicit judgment on *other* truth claims. And what is secular culture but a dizzying bazaar of competing truth claims?

But ironically, the anti-Christian-proselytizing shtick is based on self-defeating logic, because *everyone is proselytizing.*

Everyone is preaching a "gospel."

The question is *not,* Are you preaching the gospel?

It's, *What* gospel are you preaching?

The gospel of third-wave anti-racism? Or LGBTQI+ pride? Or democratic socialism? Or American nationalism? Or free-market capitalism? Or cold-water therapy or intermittent fasting or the keto diet or mindfulness or new wave psychedelics?

All of these are "gospels"—they are messages about where our hopes lie, where human history is going, what the dangers are, where salvation is to be found, where we can find community, and how to live a good life and become a good person.

Everyone is preaching *a* gospel.

Apprentices of Jesus are those who preach *his* gospel.

Now, when we say "preach the gospel," *all we mean is to tell people about Jesus:* Announce the good news of Jesus and the availability of life with him in the kingdom of God.

Again, this is what *all* people do. They talk about what they love most—fashion, music, sports, a new TV series.

We love Jesus, so we talk about Jesus.

As I said earlier, the gospel is not "If you believe in Jesus, you can go to the Good Place when you die." Mark summarizes the gospel as "The kingdom of God has come near."[33] Paul's one-line summary is "Jesus is Lord"[34] (another way of saying the same thing).

The gospel is that Jesus is the ultimate power in the universe and that life with him is now available to all. Through his birth, life, teachings, miracles, death, resurrection, ascension, and gift of the Spirit, Jesus has saved, is saving, and will save all creation. And through apprenticeship to Jesus, we can enter into this kingdom and into the inner life of God himself. We can receive and give and share in Love Loving. We can be a part of a community that Jesus is, ever so slowly, forming into a radiant new society of peace and justice that one day will co-govern all creation with the Creator, in an eternity of ever-unfolding creativity and growth and joy. And *anyone* can be a part of this story.

That's good news.

As a reaction against an unsophisticated, manipulative, and at times mean-spirited kind of "preaching," that often left people feeling degraded and demeaned, many of us have lost our sense of witness entirely. But it is *core* to our faith and essential to our discipleship that we reach out to others with this good news of Jesus.

But *how* do we announce the good news in a culture that is increasingly hostile to it?

Is it preaching on the street? Or passing out tracts that look like hundred-dollar bills? Or an IG story drip feed? Or an apologetics debate online? Or giving out C. S. Lewis books to your co-workers and praying you don't get fired?

Possibly.

But what if it could look more like cooking a meal for your neighbor? Or gently offering a prophetic word to a friend? Or inviting your co-worker along to Alpha?[35] Or an act of quiet service in your city?

All around us people are in pain. The loneliness epidemic is raging—the percentage of Americans who say they have zero close friends has quadrupled since 1990;[36] 54 percent report sometimes or always feeling that no one knows them well.[37] The digital age has us more "connected" than ever before, but sociologists tell us Gen Z is the loneliest generation of all time. We ache to be *seen,* known, and loved.

Could the way forward be as simple as meeting people in the place of pain? Isn't that what Jesus did? Could evangelism in our era look less like what Jude saw downtown and more like the stories in the Gospels?

To that end, let me offer five best practices for preaching the gospel in our secular culture.

#1 Offer hospitality

Learn to cook, set the table, and build community. (Please see the previous text starting on page 128 with "Rhythm #1: Making space for the gospel.")

#2 Find where God is already working and join him

We often start with the assumption that because someone isn't a disciple of Jesus, God isn't at work in their life. But what if we started with the opposite assumption? That God is all-present and full of love and drawn to sinners? That he is likely already at work in their life, gently inviting them in?

In this paradigm, our job is just to look for signs of the ever-present God and, when we see them (and we will), join in.

#3 Bear witness

Witness, like *disciple,* is a noun in the New Testament, not a verb. It's something you *are* before it's something you *do.* Jesus famously used this word in Acts 1:

> You will be my witnesses in Jerusalem, and in all Judea and Samaria, and to the ends of the earth.[38]

A *witness* is someone who sees or experiences something important for others to know about. Used as a verb, as in *to witness* or *to bear witness,* it just means to tell others what you saw or experienced. That's it.

We're witnesses, not salespeople. Our job is not to "close the deal" with the right technique, but simply to bear witness to our life with Jesus. Mortimer Arias, a Uraguyan scholar who served in the Methodist Church under communist persecution, put it this way:

> The kingdom is God's new order. . . . Because the new order of God is a threat to any established order, the arrival of the kingdom, forcing its way through the old order, produces a more intense reaction. It attracts and repels at the same time.[39]

Some will be attracted to the gospel, others repulsed. That's okay, we're not responsible for outcomes any more than a witness is responsible for the ruling in a trial. People have agency, free will; salvation is some kind of a mysterious mix of God's initiative and human response. Our job isn't to "save" people; it's to say with the apostle John, "We have seen, and bear witness, and declare to you" that "the life was manifested."[40]

#4 "Do the stuff"

John Wimber, the founder of the Vineyard Church, came to faith in Jesus in his twenties out of a wild background in the L.A. music scene. He read the Gospels and *Acts* and was floored by the stories of healings and prophecy and the rest. Then he came to church, where he saw *none* of it.

"When do we get to do the stuff?" he asked.[41]

"Do the stuff" has since entered the charismatic lexicon as code for operating in the manifestations of the Spirit we read of in 1 Corinthians 12—prophecy, words of wisdom and knowledge, healings, miracles, and more.

When you combine telling others about Jesus with a prophetic word, experience of healing, or insight no one could know apart from the Spirit (what Paul seems to mean by "a word of knowledge"), the result can be electric. Of course, there are *lots* of ways to do this terribly, but with the right training, we can learn to do this in a down-to-earth, calm, loving way.

More on this in the next chapter . . .

#5 Live a beautiful life

I love this line from the apostle Peter:

> Live such good lives among the pagans that, though they accuse you of doing wrong, they may see your good deeds and glorify God on the day he visits us.[42]

The Greek word translated "good" here is *kalos;* it can be translated "beautiful" or "lovely" or even "shapely."[43] The idea is to live
a radiant and compelling life, not hidden away in a Christian uto-
pia but "among"—*right in the thick of*—"the pagans" (not a de-
rogatory term in the ancient world).

Dr. Michael Green of Oxford, in his book *Evangelism in the Early
Church,* argues that 80 percent or more of evangelism in the
early church was done by ordinary Christians, not pastors or
Christian celebrities, and it was mostly just by explaining their
unusual way of life to their family and friends, by living in such a
way that people were drawn to the beauty of their lives.

My family and I still have a *long* way to go in this regard, but I
keep noticing this phenomenon: Whenever our secular friends
hear about (or especially see) us practicing Sabbath, doing life in
community and eating meals together weekly, staying married
through some deep valleys, or doing justice work in the city,
their eyes light up with longing. What to us is "normal"—resting,
engaging in emotionally healthy relationships, being open and
vulnerable in conversation, sharing our possessions, living below
our means, serving the poor—is increasingly alien to the watching world.

Do not underestimate the raw power of simply practicing the
Way of Jesus in community.

I haven't quoted from Dallas Willard in a few pages, so let me
make up for lost time:

> There is a special evangelistic work to be done, of
> course, and there are special callings to it. But if those

in the churches really are enjoying fullness of life, evangelism will be unstoppable and largely automatic. The local assembly, for its part, can then become an academy where people throng from the surrounding community to learn how to *live*. It will be a school of life (for a disciple is but a pupil, a student) where all aspects of that life seen in the New Testament records are practiced and mastered under those who have themselves mastered them through practice. Only by taking this as our immediate goal can we intend to carry out the Great Commission.[44]

Of course, all of the above will require a kind of death from us. In Greek, the word for "witness" is *martus,* from which we also get the word *martyr.*[45] Because in the early centuries of the Jesus movement, a witness and a martyr were virtually synonymous. For us in the democratic West, literal death is not an imminent threat, but there is a kind of death involved if we bear witness to Jesus' gospel—a death to our reputation as cool or sophisticated or on trend, a death to others' moral estimation of us, a possible death to our career ambitions, and more. To bear witness in our day often means we choose shame. But this is a *small* price to pay compared to "knowing Christ Jesus my Lord."[46]

You see, it's easy for a lot of us (and I'm writing to myself here) to kind of fudge this part of our apprenticeship to Jesus. I'm down for formation, emotional health, contemplative prayer—sign me up. But preaching the gospel? I think I'll just mow my neighbor's lawn and hope they figure out Jesus rose from the dead.

But if we curb this impulse of the Spirit deep within our spirits—to go, to preach the gospel, to testify—then we will "quench the Spirit"[47] in ways that will sabotage our formation and suppress our spiritual vitality. Because there is a kind of spiritual law to the universe: To possess God, we must give him away. As the missionary Frank Laubach said it, "I must talk about God, or I cannot keep Him in my mind. I must give Him away in order to have Him."[48] Otherwise, our faith will devolve to a private, individualized coping therapy and our spirituality will wither on the vine.

This is the secret law of the kingdom.

Do you know someone who is far from God? What face is coming to mind even now as you read? Whom has God put in your life to love and serve? Where has God placed you in relationship with people who are lost?

If you want more of God, give him away.

Rhythm #3: Demonstrating the gospel

Jesus did not just *preach* the gospel of the kingdom; he *embodied* it.

Word *and* deed.

Wherever Jesus went, the kingdom went.

Hospitality is a great example. The Hebrew prophets likened the coming kingdom to a feast where all God's people, Jew and Gentile alike, would gather at the table with Abraham in a new community of peace and justice. Jesus embodied this vision, one meal at a time. His eating meals with "sinners" wasn't a *picture* of salvation—it *was* salvation. As Jesus said over dinner with Zacchaeus, "Today salvation has come to this house."[49]

We talked about previous generations of Christians' well-meaning but fatally flawed reading of the miracle stories after the Enlightenment. A *better* way to read the dramatic stories of Jesus is *as signs of the in-breaking kingdom of God.* Jesus healing the sick, delivering the demonized, feeding the hungry, standing up to injustice—this is all what Isaiah and the prophets said would happen when the kingdom finally arrived.

The German theologian Jürgen Moltmann argued that miracles are not an intrusion into the "natural" order but the *healing* of it. We are so used to death, disease, injustice, and chaos that we forget—*they* are the intruders in God's good world. Moltmann wrote:

> When Jesus expels demons and heals the sick, he is driving out of creation the powers of destruction, and is healing and restoring created beings who are hurt and sick. The lordship of God to which the healings witness, restores creation to health. Jesus' healings are not supernatural miracles in a natural world. They are the only truly "natural" thing in a world that is unnatural, demonized and wounded.[50]

To follow Jesus isn't just to *watch* him do things like heal the sick and deliver the oppressed; it's to train under him to do those kinds of things too.

Now, Jesus and his original disciples did a lot of signs to demonstrate the kingdom, but there are four we see them do regularly.

Disclaimer: Each of these signs could *easily* fill an entire book; I'm just trying to spark your interest, nothing more . . .

#1 Healing

Jesus quickly became known all over Israel as a healer. People would bring the sick from miles around, literally digging through rooftops or screaming from the side of the road for his healing touch. Matthew wrote, "People soon began bringing to him all who were sick. And whatever their sickness or disease, or if they were demon possessed or epileptic or paralyzed—he healed them all."[51]

Then we see the *same pattern* in the early church.

At one point, people are healed by simply falling under Peter's shadow;[52] others recover after touching Paul's clothing.[53] And while we don't see the same *level* of power on display in ordinary disciples as we do in the apostles, James commands the church to "pray for each other so that you may be healed" because "the prayer of a righteous person is powerful and effective."[54]

Do you know anyone who is ill?[55]

#2 Deliverance

Everywhere Jesus went, he exposed the demonic powers lurking in the shadows. It's like his presence drew them into the light and his power drove them away.

Same with the disciples in *Acts*.

This is possibly the hardest "sign" for us moderns to find credible. Our secular society doesn't even believe in *God,* much less demonic beings behind phenomena as diverse as sickness, mental illness, and natural disasters.

Yet there is simply no way to make sense of Jesus' worldview without believing that our world is populated by a vast array of human *and* nonhuman beings, many of which seek to wreak havoc on God's good intentions for humanity. As the writer Luke said, "The reason the Son of God appeared was to destroy the works of the devil."[56]

And while we may see more of this in the East, the Global South, and the developing world, it's here in the "secular" West as well. In fact, with globalization, the West is becoming less and less secular. To speak of demons might still get you laughed at, but to talk about "dark spiritual energy" around a home or even a person is now considered somewhat legitimate.

And this stuff is *real,* I'm telling you. Sure, some of it is make believe or worse, paranoia. But a lot of it is genuine. My own wife was dramatically delivered, under the care of an older, mature disciple of Jesus, from a four-generation-old demonic curse. It's a long, incredible story straight out of the New Testament.[57] This experience opened our eyes to what's been hiding in plain sight: All around us people are suffering under demonization—what if we could set them free?

#3 Prophecy

Jesus clearly had access to information that could not be deduced through normal human means, not just about the future but also about people's hidden secrets ("The man you are now living with is not your husband")[58] and deepest fears ("Neither this man nor his parents sinned").[59] Of course, many people explain this with the "he was God" rationale. See above. The problem is, again, you see Jesus' disciples do this all through the New Testament, and *not* just the apostles.

The apostle Paul called this "prophecy," and he seemed to assume (and I'm thinking of 1 Corinthians 12–14 here) that the same Spirit that was on Moses and Jesus and all the prophets is now on *us,* and that, in a similar, though less potent way, we can speak a word to others from God. This rarely means we hear an audible voice from the sky; normally it's simply a feeling or a thought that comes to mind—a word, phrase, scripture, or picture . . . We then get to humbly offer that word or impression to others, in love.

Again, learning to do this well will require *training.* Examples of it going badly are rife. But once prophecy becomes a part of your life, there's no going back.

Just the other day, I was in the throes of a major decision, praying to God for clear direction. *As I was praying,* I got a message from a friend on the other side of the world with a "word" he felt was of the Spirit for me. It was *uncanny.* The language and the imagery he used were all *straight* out of my prayer time, and he had no clue I was even making a decision.

He offered a word; I interpreted it as a *word from God.*

That's the possibility of prophecy.

#4 Justice

It's a great tragedy that the word *justice* has been caught up in the culture wars and the polarizing vitriol between Left and Right. For some, justice is *the* ultimate good; for others, a pariah. Of course, *justice* means different things to different people.[60] (Think of how it's used in *Isaiah,* versus on Twitter, versus in a Clint Eastwood western.) But this is *not* a word we can let secularism define (to my friends on the Left), nor is it a practice we can abandon (to my friends on the Right). Because it's central to the heart of God.

Jesus stands in a long line of Hebrew prophets who stand for justice in the world. The most dramatic example is Jesus' cleansing of the temple, which had become a breeding ground for corruption and complicity with the empire rather than a place of overlap between heaven and earth. Jesus "put it to rights," as the Brits say. That's what justice is—making wrong things right, crooked things straight. Dr. Gerry Breshears said, "Practicing justice is an act of joining God in seeing that the created order (people and everything else) receives what it is due."[61] And doing this no matter the pain to yourself.

It means disadvantaging yourself for the *advantage* of the "other," the one in need of care.

To follow Jesus is to stand *with* him, for justice.

So,

healing,

deliverance,

prophecy,

justice.

If all this sounds next to impossible, remember that the only way we can do *any* of this stuff is "in the power of the Holy Spirit." Yes, we train under Jesus, but these aren't skills we master through the right technique (though skill is often required); they are signs of the in-breaking kingdom that we channel through our bodies in love.

Every person we meet is a God opportunity—to love and to serve.

Every day is full of possible miracles.

Every moment is pregnant with possibility, if only we open our eyes.

As Kallistos Ware put it, "From this hour and moment I can start to walk through the world, conscious that it is God's world, that he is near me in everything that I see and touch, in everyone whom I encounter."[62]

Jesus' famous last words, "Go into all the world,"[63] are written in a unique verb tense; a more literal translation would be "*As you are going* into all the world . . ." For some, this is a call to get on planes and travel to unreached people groups, but for most of us, it's simply a call to walk across the street, ride one's bike down the block, or make eye contact with the grocery checker.

As you are going about your ordinary life, live with your eyes wide open to *see* what the Father is doing, all around you, and then to partner with him. As Jesus said, "I only do what I see the Father doing."[64] Jesus had this uncanny ability to *see* people—to see what God was doing in them, right then, right there—and to unleash God's power and purposes for them in each moment.

To see like Jesus will likely require that we slow down, that we become present to the moment, that we breathe.

And as we breathe, we look for where the Father is at work and join in.

"The joyous burdens of love"

This may all sound a bit overwhelming.

We live in the age of anxiety; most of us are already burned out, overtaxed, and stressed. Now we're realizing that to be a good apprentice of Jesus we should be out practicing hospitality, telling others about Jesus, even healing the sick and casting out demons?

Deep breath.

In . . .

Out . . .

There's a word picture in the apostle Paul's writings that I find especially helpful in this regard. He called the church "the body of Christ,"[65] the embodied presence of Christ in the world. As Saint Teresa of Avila put it,

> Christ has no body on earth but yours. Yours are the eyes with which he looks compassionately on this world. Yours are the feet with which he walks to do good. Yours are the hands with which he blesses all the world. Christ has no body now on earth but yours![66]

But in Paul's theology, *we* are the body—not you, not me . . .

Us, together.

The implication is: No one person can do all this.

I love this from Thomas Kelly:

> The Loving Presence does not burden us equally with all things, but considerately puts upon each of us just a few central tasks, as emphatic responsibilities. For each of us these special undertakings are our share in the joyous burdens of love. We cannot die on *every* cross, nor are we expected to.[67]

God's heart is universal, literally—it's for all of the universe. Our hearts are not universal. We're finite, mortal, a vapor. But on each of us, Jesus will lay one small part of his universal heart of love. We will find our hearts drawn to *particular* justice issues, people groups, neighbor families, or lines of work. And it will feel like joy.

Kelly also said, "By inner persuasions He draws us to a few very definite tasks, *our* tasks, God's burdened heart particularizing His burdens in us."[68] This makes me think of the apostle Paul's line about how "the Lord has assigned to each his task."[69]

What is Christ trying to express to the watching world through your particular life?

What's your task?

Your "joyous burden of love"?

There are two primary arenas where we normally work out these energies of love.

The first is our work.

All of us work, and most of us get paid for it, though not all (parenting is a great example). In fact, this is where we spend the majority of our lives—not in praying or studying the Bible but in working at the office or on the jobsite or in the field.

Jesus himself worked in obscurity as a builder for many years. He could just as well have been a software engineer or an artist or on the city council. He could have done what *you* do.

A growing number of followers of Jesus are coming to see their work not as a J-O-B, but as a "calling" or even a "ministry." Once you adopt this mindset, it changes everything. As the preeminent preacher Tony Evans put it, "You have not really lived until you have found your God-given ministry. To live without a sense of divine appointment is to simply exist, to be detached from an eternal perspective and, therefore, simply marking time."[70]

The way we turn our work from "marking time" into "ministry" isn't by becoming a pastor or starting a nonprofit; it's by doing whatever we do the way we imagine Jesus would do it if he were *us*—with skill, diligence, integrity, humility, the kingdom's ethics, and so on.

It's also by doing our work *very* well.

Work at its best is an expression of love. As the poet Kahlil Gibran put it, "Work is love made visible."[71] If you're a chef, the way you love people through your work is by cooking the best meal you possibly can. If you're an airline pilot, it's by getting people safely home. If you're an entrepreneur, it's by starting a well-run business that contributes to the common good.

This is true not only of the high-class jobs most of us just dream about, but of *all* jobs. As Dr. Martin Luther King Jr. so beautifully said,

> Whatever your life's work is, do it well. . . . If it falls your lot to be a street sweeper, sweep streets like Michelangelo painted pictures, like Shakespeare wrote poetry, like Beethoven composed music; sweep streets so well that all the host of Heaven and earth will have to pause and say, "Here lived a great street sweeper, who swept his job well."[72]

Work well; love well.

The second arena is what the New Testament calls "good works." These are more sporadic acts of love that range from healing the sick to helping carry an elderly lady's groceries. I think of Jesus' call on his apprentices:

> Let your light shine before others, that they may see
> your *good deeds* and glorify your Father in heaven.[73]

Is there something—anything—that you feel the Spirit of God stirring in your heart?

A desire to do *good*?

Not a guilt trip or sense of religious obligation to be more involved in this or that project, but an inner prompting of the heart to some small act of kindness?

It's highly likely that's your joyous burden of love. It's easy and light. Do it, and you will discover true happiness.

Jesus knows from personal experience the emotional weight of being human: "We do not have a high priest who is unable to empathize with our weaknesses."[74] In my experience, he will often gently set a small burden of love on your heart—an idea that comes to mind in prayer, an unexpected opportunity in the middle of your day—to participate in the outward flow of the Trinity's love to all.

When the moment comes, will you follow the gentle lift in your heart?

Goal #3 may sound at odds with the previous two. *Be with Jesus* and *Become like him* can skew a little more inward, but *Do as he did* is unmistakably outward. And there is a tension, for sure, between "the contemplative life," as earlier generations called it, and "the active life." But it's a healthy tension, a both-and.

After all, the opposite of contemplation is not *action* but *reaction*.

It's not a life that is active—doing good in the world, working hard, serving those in need. That's exactly what you would expect to come from a life of abiding: fruit. The opposite of contemplation is a life that is *reactive*—getting sucked into the tyranny of the urgent instead of the important, chasing the latest fad, wasting our fleeting lives climbing some illusory corporate ladder, hurrying from one distraction to the next . . .

No, by far the hardest option but the most life-giving path forward is a life of contemplative action or active contemplation. A life of both-and, where *all* we are is integrated into apprenticing Jesus, our center, our life.

Now . . .

We're finally ready for the million-dollar question:

How do we do it?

Practicing the Way—

How? A
Rule of Life

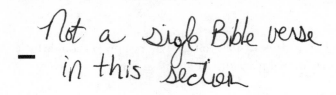
Not a single Bible verse in this section

I dream of someday visiting Japan. I'm fascinated by the culture, the art and design, the history. It's going to happen; I can feel it. But for my dream to become a reality, I need more than a vision of the beauty of Japanese culture and a desire to experience it firsthand; I need to set dates, book a flight, arrange a hotel, and save up money for the trip.

In short, I need a plan.

Otherwise, my desire—no matter how genuine—will never be realized.

For all of us, before we set out on any journey, we need at least two things: (1) a compelling vision of our desired destination, and (2) a plan for how to get there.

Nowhere is this more true than in the spiritual life.

Most people have a plan for their money (a budget), a plan for their time (a schedule), and all sorts of plans for their education, career, retirement, family, kid's soccer team, gym routine, and so on. But very few have a plan to be with Jesus and thoughtfully apprentice under him in such a way that over time they become the people who naturally do and say the kinds of things Jesus said and did.

Many people have a _desire_ and good intentions, but they do not have a plan, much less one that is time-tested and highly effective. But as Pete Scazzero put it, "Nurturing a growing spirituality with depth in our present-day culture will require a thoughtful, conscious, intentional plan for our spiritual lives."[1]

I love that: a "plan for our spiritual lives." ✱ *I do like this*

Now, this is *not* to say we *plan* our spiritual lives. To reiterate, we're not in control. It's to say we plan *for* our spiritual lives—we intentionally design our lives to give Jesus free rein over our formation. If we do this, a whole new level of joy becomes available.

One John Ortberg quote I keep coming back to is this:

> You must arrange your days so that you are experiencing deep contentment, joy, and confidence in your everyday life with God.[2]

Note the emphatic: *must*.

what? Is this even Possible?

We *must* arrange our days—our morning routines, our daily habits, our schedules and budgets and relationships, the entire webs of our lives—so that we are deeply enjoying everyday life with God.

This will require most of us not only to *arrange* our days, but also to *re*arrange our days—from the hurry, digital addiction, and chronic exhaustion that we've been conditioned to believe is normal when, in reality, it's truly insane.

This is one way to think about discipleship in the modern era: as a disciplined effort to slow down and make space for God to transform you.

But again, *this won't just happen.*

So, to the plan . . .

The trellis and the vine

[handwritten: never mentioned — Not Biblical.]

Let me introduce to you to a framework from the ancient church, one I deeply believe is vital for the *future* church: a Rule of Life.

The earliest apprentices of Jesus were asking the same question we are: How do we go about following Jesus in such a way that we are transformed?

The answer they came up with, in my estimation, is still the best—a Rule.

"Rule of Life" is ancient language, so it sounds odd or even off-putting to our modern ears. But to my antinomian friends, please note: It's *rule* of life (singular), not *rules* for life (plural).

The original Latin word was *regula,* where we get English words like *regular* and *regulation,* as well as *rule* and *ruler,* because it literally means a "straight piece of wood."[3] There's a debate among scholars as to *regula*'s origins, but some argue it was the word used in the ancient Mediterranean for a trellis in a vineyard. The word picture of a trellis was used very early on by teachers of the Way, who took Jesus' metaphor of the vine to its logical conclusion. Think of a vineyard. For a vine to "bear much fruit," what does it need? A trellis—a support structure to lift it off the ground and index it toward the light, give it room to breathe, and guide its growth in the desired direction. Without a trellis's support, the vine would bear a fraction of the fruit it's capable of, and the little it did bear would be highly vulnerable to disease, damage, and dangerous predators.

[handwritten margin note: Hmm..]

In the same way, for an apprentice of Jesus to abide in the vine and bear much fruit, we also need a trellis—a support structure to make space for life with God.

So, what exactly *is* a Rule of Life?

A Rule of Life is *a schedule and set of practices and relational rhythms that create space for us to be with Jesus, become like him, and do as he did, as we live in alignment with our deepest desires.* It's a way of intentionally organizing our lives around what matters most: God.

Rich Villodas said it well:

> This *rule* doesn't mean a list of rules. It's more of a set of practices, relationships, and commitments that is inspired by the Spirit for the sake of our wholeness in Christ.[4]

If you're turned off by the language of Rule (as some people are), here's a quick historical sidebar: For the first few centuries of the church, the phrases *Way of Life* and *Rule of Life* were used interchangeably. Within the New Testament itself, Paul writes of "my way of life in Christ Jesus, which agrees with what I teach everywhere in every church."[5] A few centuries later, when Latin became the lingua franca of the church, writers like Saint Benedict used the word *Rule*. But *rule, way*—same difference.

Put simply, a Rule of Life is a *plan* to follow Jesus. To stay true to one's commitment to apprentice under him.

David Brooks once defined *commitment* as "falling in love with something [or someone] and then building a structure of behavior around it for those moments when love falters."[6] That's what a Rule is—a structure of behavior to support us "when love falters," to anchor our lives in something deeper than our fleeting emotions and chaotic desires.

Whenever I officiate a wedding, I quote a line from the pastor and martyr Dietrich Bonhoeffer, who, in a letter from prison, said to a young couple on their wedding day, "Today, you are young and very much in love and you think that your love can sustain your marriage. It can't. Let your marriage sustain your love."[7]

In both marriage and life with God, it's the constraint of commitment that will create space for love to mature and real transformation to occur. We often chafe against it, but in the end, like caterpillars in the constraints of pupae, it is where we are transformed into butterflies—entirely new creatures of beauty.

You already have a Rule of Life

Here's the thing: *You already have a Rule of Life.*

It may be written or unwritten,

conscious or subconscious,

wise or foolish,

based on a long-term vision or short-term instant gratification,

moving you toward your desired destination or sabotaging your best intentions.

But . . .

Even if you've *never* heard of a Rule of Life until two minutes ago, you *have* one.

You have a way in which you live: a morning routine, a typical workday, a network of relationships, a budget, activities you spend your free time on, and so on.

The question isn't, Do you have a Rule of Life?

It's, Do you know what your Rule of Life *is*?

And is it giving you the life you want?

Is it working *for* you or *against* you?

The best way to tell is to take a kind of spiritual self-inventory;[8] an honest assessment of your life.

I love this little saying that comes from the business world: "Your system is perfectly designed to give you the results you are getting." I like to apply that maxim not to a widget factory or the bottom line on a spreadsheet but to the health and growth of our souls (or lack thereof). If your emotional life is off kilter, if you feel far from God, stressed, anxious, and chronically mad, and you're not becoming more of a person of love, then the odds are that something about the *system* of your life is poorly designed.

Because your *life* is the by-product of your *lifestyle*.

The problem is not that your Rule of Life isn't working, but that it *is*.

Francis Spufford, in his case for Christian spirituality, wrote about the feeling of waking up on a Saturday morning with a mild hangover, a bit lonely, empty and unfulfilled . . . and how at some point you have to grapple with the fact that your free choices aren't delivering the life you want. Your *freedom* is what got you here, not your constraint.[9]

A Rule of Life is an invitation to a very different definition of freedom than that of the modern world—an invitation to embrace the constraints that, if you give yourself to them, will eventually set you free.

The novelist Annie Dillard famously said, "How we spend our days is, of course, how we spend our lives."[10] But read through the lens of spiritual formation: "How we spend our days" doesn't just determine *what we do* with our one, precious, fleeting life, but *who we become.*

Picking up your phone first thing upon waking and checking social media isn't just a bad habit—it's a choice to let yourself become formed into a certain kind of person.

Spending more time reading the news than reading Scripture isn't just "wrong"—it's a choice to become more like your favorite news commentators than like Jesus.

Spending your money on yet *another* thing you don't need isn't just playing around with "disposable income"—it's feeding an appetite within you that will grow only more ravenous.

All these things we do, *do something to us.* They form us.

This is why . . .

Guarding and guiding

A Rule of Life must balance two sides of an emotional equation: It must guard, and it must guide. The Christian intellectual Andy Crouch beautifully defines a Rule of Life as "a set of practices to guard our habits and guide our lives."[11]

Let's circle back to the vine metaphor. A gardener has two jobs: tend the plants and keep out the weeds.

In the same way, each of us needs to ask, *What do I want to* put into *my life?* and *What do I want to* keep out?

Plus, *What do I want to* grow? and *What do I want to* die?

If you were to look at my Rule (one I live by with a small community of friends), you'd see a bunch of spiritual disciplines you would likely expect: an hour of quiet each morning to pray and read Scripture, a weekly Sabbath and meal with my community, a monthly day in solitude, and so on. But then you'd see a bunch of odd (but for me, keystone) habits that don't show up on any historical Rule of Life, because they are mostly my way of dealing with the dark underbelly of the digital age. Really, they are more like anti-habits, my attempt at counter-formation.

Here are a few examples:

- "Parenting" my phone. I have an old-school analog alarm clock by my bed. My phone "goes to bed" at 8:30 P.M. each night, tucked away in a drawer in my home office, and it isn't "allowed up" until I've finished my morning time of prayer and hit my daily quota for writing.

- Practicing a full twenty-four-hour digital Sabbath. We power off *all* devices, including our phones, computers, and TV, for the entirety of our weekly day of rest and worship. This goes for our teenage kids as well.[12]

- Limiting my social media use to one day a week.[13] I think of it like breathing toxic fumes—sometimes necessary to live in the modern world but no good for you, and too much will kill you.

- Limiting my intake of media (TV, film, YouTube) to a max of four hours a week. I lifted this from the Rule of Life from Andy Crouch and the community at Praxis: "Instead of having our imagination saturated by media, we seek to be transformed by the renewing of our mind. We commit to establish structured limits for our use of screens and our consumption of entertainment, in quantity, frequency, and moral character."[14] That's the stuff.

Notice: These *are* more like "rules," but the heart behind them isn't legalism. I'm well aware they aren't a measure of my spiritual maturity at all. (If anything, my need for them is a measure of my *immaturity*.) Not one of them makes me any more loving or holy; I just recognize the power of things like technology and media to both form and *deform* me. Left unchecked, these things are *designed* to consume my life and shape me into a specific kind of person——one who is wildly unlike Jesus. But my deepest desire is for *God* to consume my life and, in time, shape me into *his* image.

And while I'm *not* saying you need to adopt the same rules I have, I very much believe we *all* need at least *some* rules around our phones and, should we choose to play with fire, social media.

Does that grate on you? Are you thinking, *But I'm a free spirit; I don't like to be controlled!*

I hate to break it to you, but: You *are* being controlled, by your addiction to your phone, the appetites of your body for pleasure, and the spooky algorithms of Silicon Valley. Coming up with "rules" can put your life *back* under the control of your deepest desires.

Choose your own constraints, *or they will be chosen* for *you,* not by the Spirit of God stirring your own heart toward love, but by a programmer in Silicon Valley working to steal your time and shape your behavior.

The choice is yours: Rule, or be ruled.

To live by a Rule, of course, will require a crash course in learning to say *no*——not just to sin, but to all sorts of things, good and bad.

This, in turn, will require many of us to rethink our criteria for decision-making.

I used to weigh potential behaviors with the question, Is this sinful or not? But now that I better understand the gospel and its possibility of "life that is truly life" with Jesus, my new question is, Does this move me toward Jesus or away?

That's a *far* more interesting question . . .

The goal is to live with a kind of focus and intentionality and peacefulness that many admire and aspire to but precious few attain. Steve Jobs, the Californian iconoclast, famously said he was as proud of what Apple had *not* done as what the company had. He clarified, "People think focus means saying yes to the thing you've got to focus on. But that's not what it means at all. It means saying no to the hundred other good ideas that there are. You have to pick carefully."[15]

It's the same with a Rule: "You have to pick carefully."

You have to say *no* more often than *yes,* because there are only so many hours in a day, and so many days in a life.

But hear me: A wisely chosen Rule has the potential to enrich your life in ways you can't possibly imagine.

Four things a good Rule will do for you

#1 It will help you turn vision into reality

We all know the saying "The road to hell is paved with good intentions," because it captures an acute pain of the human condition. A common feature of the Fall is to aspire to a beautiful life but then fail at the commitment, discipline, and patient endurance required to turn that vision into a reality. Most of us genuinely desire what is good, but we fail because we avoid, procrastinate, or make excuses rather than take the necessary steps to move forward into our hearts' desires. "I do not do the good I want to do, but the evil I do not want to do—this I keep on doing."[16] We constantly self-sabotage.

This is the great challenge of discipleship: to move from aspirational ideas to authentic transformation.

A Rule of Life can bridge the gap. It can take aspirational ideas like *be with Jesus* or *become a person of love* or *you must ruthlessly eliminate hurry from your life* and habituate them into our bodies, literally rewiring our central nervous systems. Without a Rule, these ideas will likely devolve into sentimental cliché.

The spiritual writer John Ortberg once said to me, "Following Jesus is kind of like playing golf. The easy part is to get a vision of what you need to do—the perfect swing, the right body stance, the correct angle of approach—and, of course, make par. The *hard* part is getting that vision into your muscle memory so it just naturally comes out of you without even thinking about it."

I don't golf, but I still think about that analogy. Hearing sermons (or reading books) about following Jesus is kind of like watching YouTube videos on golf—it's a wonderful place to start, but you won't get very far until you put your shoes on and hit the green.

#2 It will help you experience peace as you live in alignment with your deepest desires

Saint Seraphim of Sarov once said, "Acquire inner peace and thousands around you will find their salvation." We all crave this inner peace, but how do we "acquire" it?

There's no one answer to this question, but the business consultant Stephen Covey once said, "We achieve inner peace when our schedule aligns with our values." Because our schedules are so often *not* aligned with our values, many of us live with this electric current of anxiety pulsing through our nervous systems all the time; it's just *there,* nagging at us and draining our energy reserves.

In "this twittering world" of the digital age, it's easier than ever to be "distracted from distraction by distraction," as T. S. Eliot once said.[17] The most powerful companies in the history of the world are working around the clock with the most sophisticated algorithms ever devised to stoke your fear and feed your anger, by any means necessary.[18]

To live a life of peace in the digital age will *demand* a kind of resistance.

A Rule of Life is just that: an act of defiance against the powers and principalities of the digital empire. A way of staying true to your deepest desires: to be with Jesus, to let him form you into a person of love, to do whatever God put you on earth to do. A way of refusing to waste your life.

Of course, the challenge of a Rule of Life is that it will force you to clarify what your deepest desires *are,* to listen to your heart and your God. One of the best ways to do that is, as an Ignatian scholar put it to me, to "pay attention to your jealousy." He meant that playfully, as in: Pay attention when you see a feature of another person's life and think, *I wish my life was like that.*

Then craft a Rule to move in that direction.

#3 It will help you live at the right pace

Pacing is everything.

Too much, too fast, and we accelerate to hurry (definition: too much to do, not enough time to do it), killing our spiritual lives, sapping our emotional energy, and inevitably burning down our soul.

But the reverse is also true: Too little, too slow, and we atrophy, falling into a lethargic, self-centered fugue—what the ancients called "acedia," or sloth, nicknamed by the monks "the noonday demon."

A Rule of Life will help you determine in advance the speed of your life, so you don't burn out or stall out, but "press on toward the goal to win the prize."[19]

#4 It will help you balance freedom and discipline

Imagine a thriving life on a pendulum: On one side is freedom; on the other, discipline.

Spontaneity and structure.

Chaos and order.

Too far toward freedom and you're racked by anxiety; too far toward discipline and you feel claustrophobic.

Depending on your personality, you will likely gravitate toward one pole or the other, and in various stages of life, you will likely undulate back and forth a bit. That's healthy. The key is a balance.

This is why it's a *Rule,* not a *law.*

Think about the difference: A law is handed down from an external source, and it has very little flexibility. It's guilt or innocence based, and it's designed to keep you away from the negative. And unless I'm missing something, my anarchist friends are just plain wrong—we *need* laws.

But a Rule is very different: It's self-generated from your internal desires, it has a *ton* of flexibility, it's relationship based (not morality based), and it's designed to index you *toward* your vision of the good life.

For example, the main road outside my neighborhood has a twenty-five miles per hour speed limit. That's a law. It doesn't matter if it's a holiday, there's no one on the road, and I'm driving a Ferrari (hypothetical situation here—my books haven't done *that* well . . .). I still have to drive no more than twenty-five miles per hour.

Compare that to a little "rule" T and I have for our marriage: We aim for twenty to thirty minutes a day of one-on-one connection, one date night a week, and a quarterly weekend getaway without the kids to just rest and be together. There's a *ton* of flexibility in our rule. And when we miss it, we don't feel guilt or shame; but we *do,* more often than not, feel more tension, more distance, less in sync, and less in love.

Hence, the rule.

It's the same with a Rule of Life: It's a map and a path, not a straitjacket.

My friend Tyler Staton uses the metaphor of an anchor on a boat: The Rule is the anchor, and your life is the boat. Most of the time, when you're living rightly, you don't even feel it; but when you drift, you feel it pull you back to center.

Margaret Guenther—wife, mother, and Anglican priest—said it so very well:

> A good rule can set us free to be our true and best selves. It is a working document, a kind of spiritual budget, not carved in stone but subject to regular review and revision. It should support us, but never constrict us.[20]

To close, I must say this: There is no one-size-fits-all approach to a Rule of Life, because there is no one-size-fits-all approach to spiritual formation. There isn't a "right" way to craft a Rule of Life any more than there is a "right" way to pray. Jesus came to set us free by living according to his Way, not to enslave us to routine, ritual, and religion.

That said, some core practices from the Way of Jesus should ideally show up, at least in some iteration, in the Rule of Life of every disciple.

But before we name them, a short word on what the practices *are* . . .

The practices defined

why renamed?

The professor Craig Dykstra of Duke Divinity School once said, "The life of the Christian faith is the practice of many practices."[21]

What I'm calling "the practices," most people call "the spiritual disciplines."[22] My friend and co-worker Strahan calls them "altars of availability." Ruth Haley Barton calls them "sacred rhythms";[23] the late pastor Eugene Peterson, "rhythms of grace";[24] Reformed theologians, "means of grace."[25] But to translate into a more secular vernacular, they are essentially habits that are based on the life (read: lifestyle) of Jesus.

Let's start with what the practices are *not*.

#1 They are not a barometer of spiritual maturity

Yes, a disciple is a "disciplined one," and yes, it's likely that a more mature disciple of Jesus will live by a rigorous regimen of practices and a less mature disciple will be more chaotic and noncommittal. *But.* Love is the metric of spiritual maturity, not discipline.

Discipline is a *means* to an *end*—to be with Jesus, become like him, and do what he did. The psychologist Rich Plass put it this way in *The Relational Soul,* "Spiritual disciplines are not an end in themselves. They are means to an end. . . . Disciplines set the soul on the path where it can come to know God and live present to others in love."[26]

Follow their logic—it's spot on: Disciplines are the path, not the destination.

I know some people who never miss a week of church, read through the entire Bible every year, and never watch R-rated movies (all good things) but who are still self-righteous, controlling, fueled by anger, blind to their own shadow, and, at times, incredibly unloving.[27] And I know others who are in a season of just trying to survive parenting little kids and barely getting ten minutes a day to pray. But tired as they may be, they are becoming more loving with each passing year.

Love is the metric to pay attention to.

#2 They are not a gloomy bore

The words *practice* and *discipline* can sound onerous, especially for more spontaneous and fun-loving personalities. But keep in mind: many of the practices are incredibly joyful—Sabbath, sleep (yes, sleep is a practice of Jesus), feasting, gratitude, celebration, worship, etc. And many others, like solitude or fasting or serving, *become* joyful as we practice them over time.

As Richard Foster said, "Joy is the keynote of all the Disciplines."[28]

#3 They are not a form of merit

While I imagine that God the Father is delighted at any effort we make to move in his direction, we're not earning *anything* by practicing Sabbath or reading Scripture or serving the poor—and certainly not by some merit-based judicial ledger.

This is especially important to say for those from more legalistic backgrounds. John Ortberg said it well: "People who live under the bondage of legalism and then hear the message of grace are sometimes leery that talk of disciplines might lead to another form of religious oppression. But spiritual disciplines are simply a means of appropriating or growing toward the life that God graciously offers."[29]

"Appropriating"—that is a very good word.

#4 They are not the Christian version of virtue signaling

Cue the common trope of posting online not because you actually believe in something but because you just want to stay #ontrend, look good, and avoid cancel culture; social justice as fast fashion meets the new classism.

Jesus was aware of this subtle trap and spoke forcefully against it. The one time he specifically taught on the practices,[30] he named three (prayer, fasting, and generosity), and while he gave insight into each discipline, the thrust of his message was a *warning* about the dangers of practicing "to be seen by others."

There seems to be a kind of spiritual law at work in our formation: If you do the practices for the wrong reasons (to look good, one-up, or mask your shame), they work *against* your formation, not for it; they become a kind of parasitic infestation on your soul.

There are dangers all along the spiritual path. It's still the right path to follow, but they are real dangers.

Finally . . .

#5 They are not a means of control

We can easily be deluded into thinking of the practices as something we *do* to get the results we desire in our emotional and spiritual lives; they then become (futile) attempts to manipulate the symptoms of our lives to avoid pain.

But there is *no* escaping pain.

The practices are how we meet God *in* our pain and deepen our surrender to him, trusting God to do what he will, when he will.

So, that said, what *are* the practices?

The practices are disciplines based on the lifestyle of Jesus that create time and space for us to access the presence and power of the Spirit and, in doing so, be transformed from the inside out.

To better understand what a "spiritual" discipline is, it may help to clarify what a discipline is in general. Here's a standard definition:

A discipline is any activity I can do by direct effort that will eventually enable me to do what I currently cannot do by direct effort.

Let me illustrate with an athletics metaphor: I wasn't much of an athlete as a kid, but I was still obsessed with basketball. (Go, Warriors!) I remember spending *hours* dribbling and shooting drills, setting up cones in my driveway, staying out until dark working on my shot. Because, intuitively, I knew the way to become a good basketball player was not to *try* hard but to *train* hard. It was thousands of hours of *practice*. The more I did what I *could* do—dribbling exercises, shooting drills, and so on—the more I became the kind of person who was learning to do what I could *not* do at that point: slay on the court.

In my case, the analogy breaks down due to an unfortunate mix of genetics and late neuromuscular development, *but* the word picture is sound.

What drills are to basketball (or scales are to playing the guitar, or a sprint workout is to a half marathon, or shading spheres is to an artist), the practices are to becoming a person of love. We do what we *can* do—read Scripture, pray, practice Sabbath, eat a meal with community—to be formed into people who can *eventually* do what we *currently* cannot do: live and love like Jesus.

A discipline is a way to access power.

A *spiritual* discipline is a way to access not just your own power (through a kind of resistance training of your willpower muscle) but also *God's* power. Spiritual disciplines are the Jesus-designed way of offering yourself to God so that you can draw on (or "appropriate") what the apostle Paul called "grace"[31]—the empowering presence of God's Spirit.

Here's Willard again:

> The disciplines are activities of mind and body purposefully undertaken, to bring our personality and total being into effective cooperation with the divine order. They enable us more and more to live in a power that is, strictly speaking, beyond us, deriving from the spiritual realm itself, as we "yield ourselves to God, as those that are alive from the dead, and our members as instruments of righteousness unto God."[32]

Put another way, they are *our* part in transformation.

Ancient Christians called this "synergy"—working not *for* God, but *with* God.

God works, *and* we work.

God has a part, and we have a part.

Our part is to slow down, make space, and surrender to God; *his* part is to transform us—we simply do not have that power. Utilizing the disciplines, we can say with Paul, "God is working in [me], giving [me] the desire and the power to do what pleases him."[33]

Jesus modeled a set of core practices that we will cover next: disciplines like Sabbath, Scripture, prayer, and fasting. Scholars call them the "classical disciplines"—not just because they date back to the ancient world but because they are the core disciplines for following Jesus, for *all people,* for *all time.*

But it must be said: *Anything* can become a spiritual discipline if we offer it to God as a channel of grace.

Example: For years I resisted getting a family dog. (To quote my doctor, I have "obsessive tendencies"; i.e., I'm *extremely* clean. . . . Dogs, not so much.) But finally, it was me against the entire family, and no surprise, I lost. Enter Jyn Erso. (Yes, named after the Star Wars heroine. I voted to name her Chewy—who says that's not a unisex name? The Wookie version of Alex or Taylor? But again, I lost.[34]) At first, she drove me nuts. As if a house with three kids wasn't stressful enough! But I realized it was time to embrace what *is* ("If you can't beat 'em, . . ."), so I started taking her on walks in the forest near our Portland home and just offering those walks to God and asking him to free me of my perfectionism, controlling spirit, and chronic anger, all of which block the flow of love. Surprisingly, to me, I fell in love with Jyn. Still a long way to go on the perfectionism, but we're moving in the right direction. . . .

It could be walking your dog to let go of perfectionism, taking a spin class to care for your body, visiting an elderly neighbor who is lonely, driving in the slow lane, reading philosophy, or writing a proof for physics—you can offer any of these activities to God in hope that he will fill those spaces with his transforming presence.

Dr. Robert Mulholland defines spiritual disciplines as "acts of loving obedience by which we offer our brokenness and bondage to God for healing and liberation."[35]

The practices aren't everything, but they are really, *really* important.[36] They are non-negotiable for those who desire to be with and become like Jesus. They will not carry us all the way down the path in our formation, but they are how we begin. And like dribbling drills in basketball, we never mature beyond them.

This is what it means to "follow" Jesus—it means we adopt his overall Way of life.

And the good news is that transformation *is* possible, *if* we are willing to arrange (or rearrange) our lives around the practices, rhythms, and truths that Jesus himself did.

In his incarnation, Jesus laid down the pattern for how to flourish as a human being in God's world. Jesus himself was an embodied soul, with the plasticity of a central nervous system. His time-tested practices show us the Way; they attune us to God and allow the Spirit to heal and save us. Our job is just to offer them back to God for the only pure motive there is: joyful love.

As we do so, the automatic responses of sin in our bodies are slowly (but surely) re-habituated and removed, we begin to "naturally" live out the teachings of Jesus in our everyday lives, and God becomes more and more real to us as we are drawn into the Trinity's inner life of love.

Is there any better way to live?

The nine

There's no official list of the practices of Jesus, because any habit you see in Jesus' life would count—walking in nature, climbing a mountain, washing feet. None of these show up on a classical list of the spiritual disciplines, yet each one could be utilized by an apprentice of Jesus for formation.

At Practicing the Way, we recommend you design your Rule of Life to integrate the following nine core practices.

A short word on each . . .

#1 Sabbath

The spiritual journey begins with rest. You see this on the first page of the Bible, where the day begins at sundown, with sleep, and the week begins on Sabbath, with rest.

When I offer spiritual direction to people, I often begin by prescribing sleep, margin, time off work—rest. Because chronically exhausted, sleep-deprived, overbusy people are *not* loving, peaceful, and full of joy.

Rest is *essential* to apprenticeship under Jesus.

Tiredness is an unavoidable feature of life this side of eternity, but so many of us operate at a *dangerous* level of tired, so much that we can't sense God's presence or hear his voice.

Sabbath is an entire day of your week—one-seventh of your life—set aside to not only stop and rest but also delight in and worship the God who made you to be with himself. It's a day to cultivate joy in a world of sadness. As Nan Fink said in her memoir *Stranger in the Midst,*

> Shabbat is like nothing else. Time as we know it does not exist during these twenty-four hours, and the worries of the week soon fall away. A feeling of joy appears. The smallest object, a leaf or a spoon, shimmers in a soft light, and the heart opens. Shabbat is a meditation of unbelievable beauty.[37]

In ugly times, we need the Sabbath to keep our hearts alive to the beauty of God and life with him in his world.

#2 Solitude

Most of the great ones of the Way all agree: Solitude is *the most foundational* of *all* the practices of Jesus.

Again, Nouwen wrote, "Without solitude it is virtually impossible to live a spiritual life."[38]

And solitude has an unspoken but ever-present companion: silence. James Connor wrote that silence is the "one door into communion with God."[39] While it may not be the *one* door, all the masters of the Way agree that the practice of solitude and silence—what the Gospel writers call the *erēmos* or "the quiet place"—is utterly key.

Once we are rested, the quiet is where we go to find God. Because it's there, in the quiet, that the inner roar of our world of noise—the distraction, the chaos, and all the lies—fades away, and what shimmers in its place is the peace and presence of God.

Centuries ago, Saint Isaac the Syrian said, "Speech is the organ of the present world. Silence is the mystery of the world to come."[40] In silence, we enter into the mystery of the world to come—and into God himself.

Find the quiet to find God.

#3 Prayer

Jesus didn't go into "the quiet place" because he was an introvert who needed a little me time; he went there to pray.[41]

Many people hear *prayer* and think of one particular *type* of prayer—asking God for things, which is perfectly legitimate. But I mean *prayer* in the broader scope of the word, as *the medium through which we communicate and commune with God.*

There are four basic levels of prayer[42] (or, you could say, dimensions to prayer):

1. **Talking to God**—praying premade prayers like the psalms or liturgy, or singing prayers at church, and so on

2. **Talking with God**—conversing with God about your life. Lifting up the details of your life before God with gratitude (talking to him about what is *good* in your life and world), lament (talking to him about what is *evil* in your life and world), and petition and intercession (calling on God to fulfill his promises to *overcome evil with good*)

3. **Listening to God**—hearing God's voice through quiet listening, Lectio Divina, the prophetic, and more

4. **Being with God**—just looking at God, looking at you, in love (also called "contemplative prayer")

All four types of prayer are essential to cultivate a loving relationship with God. But many people never move beyond the first two types of prayer, and even fewer discover the joy and possibility of the fourth.

Of course, prayer is not a linear, four-step formula; it's more like a long and winding road we travel over a lifetime. The key is to just stay on the path. As Ronald Rolheiser put it,

There is no bad way to pray and there is no one starting point for prayer. All the great spiritual masters offer only one non-negotiable rule: You have to show up for prayer and you have to show up regularly.[43]

#4 Fasting

Fasting is one of the most essential and powerful of all the practices of Jesus and, arguably, the single most neglected in the modern Western church.

In fasting, you are literally praying with your body, offering *all* that you are to God in worship. As you yield your body to God, you are breaking the power of the flesh to control you and opening up to the power of the Spirit in its place.

You are learning to be joyful, *even when you don't get what you want.* You are practicing suffering and, through it, increasing your capacity for joy in all circumstances.

And you are amplifying your prayers—increasing your capacity to both hear and be heard by God.

Fasting is *hard,* especially at first. Though it grows much easier with regular practice. But the "hangry" feelings that come up when we forgo meals often expose the arenas of our soul most in need of grace—and, again, open us to God in surprising ways. We begin to feed on what Jesus called the "food to eat that you know nothing about."[44]

Fasting truly is a lost discipline whose time has come.

#5 Scripture

Scripture is the primary way we are "transformed by the renewing of [our] mind."[45] As we think God's thoughts after him, we begin to develop the "mind of Christ."[46]

We begin to see the world as he sees it.

Think how he thinks.

Feel what he feels.

As we curate the flow of our consciousness to intentionally mirror that of Christ, we increasingly live in the joy and peace and love *of* Christ.

There are all sorts of ways to read Scripture—slowly and prayerfully, all alone (a practice called "Lectio Divina"), out loud in large swaths with our community (how most of Scripture was designed to be experienced), in deep study in a classroom, while sitting under teaching or preaching in church, through memorization, and more.[47] All work together to fill, form, and free our minds.

#6 Community

John Ortberg has observed, "We generally sin alone, but we heal together."[48] Or as they say in AA: "*I* get drunk, *we* stay sober."

The church is where we are re-parented into the family of God; it's scary because it regularly goes wrong (examples abound). Our deepest wounds come from relationships, and yet, so does our deepest healing.

But we simply are not meant to follow Jesus alone. The radical individualism of Western culture is not only a mental health crisis and growing social catastrophe; it's a death blow to any kind of serious formation into Christlike love. Because it's *in* relationships that we are formed and forged.

From coming together on Sunday for worship to eating a meal around a table to practicing confession to entering into spiritual direction, therapy, or mentorship—community is how we travel the Way, together.

Do you have your traveling companions?

#7 Generosity

As we slow down and arrange our lives around their center in Jesus, this new simplicity of life will, in turn, enable generosity, the giving of our extra resources to God and those in need. Once you are living *under* your means rather than chronically overextended, it opens up all sorts of new possibilities.

This is one of *the most joyful* of all the practices.

At the heart of the Trinitarian community we call God is an outflow of generous, self-giving, forgiving love. In the gospel itself, "God so loved the world that he *gave* his one and only Son," and the Son, in turn, *gave* the Spirit.[49] When we give—our money, our resources, our time and love—we get to participate in that divine outflow of love. And "when you act like God, you get to feel like God."[50]

It comes as no surprise that sociologists are just now discovering the truth of what Jesus said two millennia ago: "It is happier to give than to receive."[51]

What do you have to give?

Put another way: How badly do you want joy?

#8 Service

Jesus explained his life this way: "The Son of man did not come to be served, but to serve, and to give his life as a ransom for many . . ."[52]

My default setting is the opposite; I want to *be* served, not *to* serve . . .

Can you imagine what the world would be like if people were to actually live this way?

Think of the raging epidemic of injustice in modern society— the racism, bigotry, and political polarization, or the growing chasm of inequality between the rich and poor, the haves and have-nots. Sociologists tell us our society is more divided than it's been since the Civil War.

How do we possibly heal these wounds?

We serve.

This could be quietly befriending the poor in your city or volunteering for a local nonprofit, but it could also be parenting your two-year-old or caring for your aging parents.

Every day is *full* of opportunities to follow Jesus' example, and give your life in service.

And here's a key truth: Not only does the practice of service have the potential to mend our fractured world; it has the power to mend *us*. This is one of the most surprising things about the discipline. You think you're there to help others, but you quickly realize *you're* the one being helped. You're being set free of your ego, your entitlement, your self-obsession. When you serve in the Way of Jesus, the lines blur between servant and served, giver and recipient. *Both* give, and both receive. Dignity is restored in one; freedom won in the other.

In one of the final stories of Jesus' life, Jesus takes on the garb of a servant and insists on washing his apprentices' feet. This is Jesus *intentionally* taking the lower social position, the master trading places with the servant. Then Jesus quietly says this: "I have set you an example that you should do as I have done for you. . . . Now that you know these things, you will be blessed if you do them."[53]

Do you want to be blessed?

#9 Witness

Jesus' final words to his apprentices were, "Go into all the world and *preach the gospel* to all creation."[54]

Again, our role *isn't* to "convert" anyone, but it *is* to preach—to tell others the good news of Jesus, through the practice of witness.

To do this, we must become a people of hospitality in a culture of hostility. We must embody and extend the love, welcome, warmth, and generosity of the inner life of God.[55] We must open our homes, our tables, and our lives to "the last, the least, and the lost."[56]

I may not be able to solve the great systemic injustices of our time, but I can cook some of the best pizza you've ever had and invite you to my table.

Who knows what else could come of that?

A Rule of Life for the modern world—a Christian spirituality in the age of smartphones, Wi-Fi, and rising political polarization—is the holy grail of our time.

Together, these nine core practices from the Way of Jesus form a time-tested trellis that is conducive to deep inner healing and overall life transformation. And that *can be done* in our day.

Do you have a trellis?

If not, are you ready to build one?

A few tips

Okay, a few tips for crafting your Rule of Life. This is still a new concept for a lot of us, and a little guidance may be in order.

#1 Start where you are, not where you "should" be

In our zeal, it's hard to not overreach and attempt to live like a monk from day one. This is a strategy doomed to fail. Margaret Guenther called it "first week of Lent syndrome."[57] Unrealistic goals just leave us discouraged and disillusioned.

For most people, the hardest work of designing a Rule of Life is simply getting started. Because to craft a Rule, you have to be *very* honest about where you are in your discipleship and what you're capable of in this season. You must name your limits—emotionally, relationally, even spiritually—and from there determine what you honestly can do, and then, *let that be enough.*

Step one: We must find God in the contours of our actual lives—not the lives we wish we had, used to have, or plan to have, but the lives we *actually* have, here, now. Because "God has yet to bless anyone except where they actually are."[58]

If you're just beginning, start small, with joyful, easily attainable practices—what the Stanford behavioral scientist BJ Fogg called "tiny habits."[59] Yes, an hour a day in prayer is ideal, but don't start there, especially if you have kids or a demanding job. Start with ten or fifteen minutes; pray a psalm, go on a short walk, breathe.

If that's too much, start with *five* minutes.

Still too much? Start with *one.*

And make it what many "serious" Christians view as anathema—*fun*. Dare to ask yourself, *How do I enjoy God?* Is it sipping tea by the window early in the morning? Getting together with other followers of Jesus to throw a party? Walking in the forest?

Start *there* . . .

#2 Think subtraction, not addition

Let me say it *again:* Following Jesus is not about doing *more,* but doing *less.*

It's tempting to make your Rule of Life a list of things to *do*—and that's not all bad. But for most of us, it's just as important, if not more so, to focus on what we're *not* going to do, to build margin into the architecture of our lives.

Some teachers separate practices of "engagement" (disciplines of *doing* like justice, worship, study, and so on) from practices of "abstinence" (disciplines of *not doing* like Sabbath, silence, fasting, and so on). In certain cultural contexts, practices of engagement are necessary to break people out of lethargy and laziness. But if, like me, you live in a city, have a young family and a demanding job, and are constantly fighting off hurry—then practices of *abstinence* become the need of the hour.

Take *out* more than you put *in.*

Less is more.

#3 Take a balanced approach

You can plot the practices of Jesus along four axis points: disciplines you do alone and those you do in community, and as I just said, disciplines of engagement and of abstinence.

Alone/Community and Abstinence/Engagement

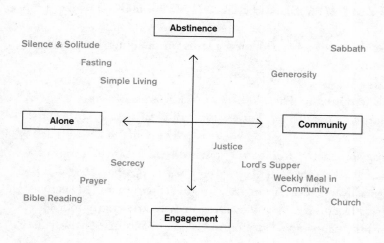

Most people hear the phrase *spiritual disciplines* and think of the alone/abstinence quadrant, but the community/engagement dimension is just as important.

Based on your personality, you'll likely gravitate toward one quadrant; that's fine. Just make sure there's a balance in your Rule.

#4 Take into account your personality and spiritual temperament

Work *with* your personality, not against it. If you're more introverted and intellectual, carve out plenty of time to be alone, read, and think. If you're more extroverted and action oriented—go *do* stuff with other people.

Yes, we need a balanced approach, but some of us need *way* more of certain practices than others. A little community goes a long way for me, but I need a ton of time in the quiet. For others, it's the reverse.

Please hear me: There's *so* much space to be who you are before God.

The spiritual writer Gary Thomas developed the concept of a "spiritual temperament" in his book *Sacred Pathways,* which is essentially a personality theory for prayer. He wrote, "There is great freedom in how we can meet with and enjoy God. This is by his design and according to his good pleasure." His warning: "Beware of narrowing your approach to God."[60]

He categorized nine spiritual temperaments, each with its own unique pathway to God:

1. **Naturalists:** loving God in nature and the outdoors

2. **Sensates:** loving God with the senses—candles, incense, materials, and so on

3. **Traditionalists:** loving God through ritual, symbolism, and liturgy

4. **Ascetics:** loving God in solitude and self-denial

5 **Activists:** loving God by fighting injustice

6. **Caregivers:** loving God by caring for those in need

7. **Enthusiasts:** loving God with music and dance and celebration

8. **Contemplatives:** loving God through quiet adoration

9. **Intellectuals:** loving God with the mind[61]

No one of these is better than the others. Tragically, we humans tend to moralize our preferences, which can cause great harm to others who are different from us. The church tradition you grew up in or were saved into may have emphasized one or two dominant pathways that are *different* from *your* preferred approach to God. To grow, you may need to expand your horizon of possibility and explore new pathways to God.

#5 Take into account your season of life and stage of discipleship

Life is all about seasons, and just as our schedules, budgets, and relationships change in various seasons of our journeys, so should our Rule of Life. If you have little kids at home, start small, be gentle with yourself, and remember that children can be like monastic bells to remind you that your time is not your own.[62] Every childlike interruption to your Rule can function as an invitation to surrender control and become a person of self-giving love.

As Tish Harrison Warren, *New York Times* columnist and mother of three, put it, "This longing for a contemplative ideal can be a particular burden for me as a young mom, in a home that is typically loud, active, sleepless, and filled with unending requests and needs."[63]

Don't fight against your season; work *with* it.

I'm also a firm believer in the psychology of stage theory. We mature through various stages in our psycho-spiritual development, just as we do in our physical development. Each one is necessary and healthy. Eventually, as you mature, you will inevitably face what the ancients called the "dark night of the soul"——a season where the practices don't "work" like they are supposed to. You still practice them, but you don't feel the same connection to God. That's part of the journey.[64]

The key is to know your season of life and stage of development and adjust your practice accordingly.

#6 Keep a healthy blend of upstream and downstream practices

The best teachers of the Way I know all utilize the practices almost like a doctor would deploy a medicine or therapy.

As a general rule, if you're struggling with a sin of *commission* (a behavior you *do* that you want to *stop* doing), you will need practices of *abstinence*. So, to overcome a porn addiction or gossip or compulsive shopping, emphasize fasting or silence or simplicity (respectively). To overcome a sin of *omission* (a behavior you *don't* do that you want to *start* doing), you will need practices of *engagement.* So, to mitigate against apathy, for example, begin serving the poor.

A few days ago, someone asked me, "How do I overcome pride?" I thought for a quick minute, then recommended they practice community, serving, and solitude; these are the three best disciplines I know to partner with God to cultivate a spirit of humility.

By *downstream* disciplines I just mean the practices that you naturally love and find joy in. And by *upstream,* I mean those practices that feel harder for you (and possibly, less pleasant) but move your soul toward growth. As a general rule, we need only a few upstream practices and a *lot* of downstream practices.

The key is: We need *both.*

Of course, we all hate this, but the practices that are the hardest for us will likely be the most transformative. It's just like the exercise mantra: *Follow the pain.*

Yet at the same time (and we must embrace the both-and here), *follow your joy.*

#7 Follow the J curve

Learning theorists point out that learning *any* new skill follows a J-shaped curve. When you attempt to grow in a new skill (from playing the piano to practicing Sabbath), you often get *worse* at it before you get better.

J Curve

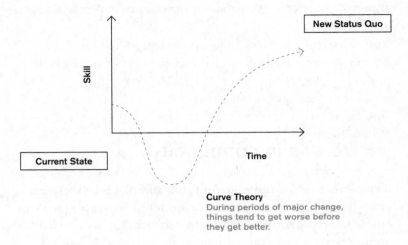

New Status Quo

Skill

Current State

Time

Curve Theory
During periods of major change, things tend to get worse before they get better.

I'll never forget when I was learning to play guitar. A year or so in, I realized that the proper picking technique is up-down, up-down, but I was playing down-down, down-down. I had to *relearn* all the fancy licks I'd been practicing, and at first, I sounded *worse*. But in time, with lots of practice, I started to sound *better*.

Similarly, you may enjoy your days off work but find yourself fidgety or anxious or bored when you begin to practice Sabbath. Or you may love a little quiet in the morning while you drink your coffee but have all sorts of painful emotions come up when you attempt solitude, silence, and stillness.

Questions will come into your mind, like *Am I doing a good job or no? Do I like it or dislike it?*

Those types of questions just aren't very helpful.

When they come up, gently set them aside. And take a deep breath. Resist the urge to judge, critique, or overthink your practice.

Just stay with it; let God do his work through the discipline. Eventually, you'll begin to feel at ease in your body with God.

Follow the J curve down and then up.

#8 Do this in community

The current micro-resurgence of Rule of Life in the Western church is a joy to my heart. Unfortunately, it's mostly being run through the grid of Western-style individualism, with individual people writing *their* Rule of Life.

For the record, this is *not* a bad thing. As we've said, you already have a Rule; this is just bringing more intentionality to your life. I'm all for it. Onward.

But you should know this: Historically, a Rule of Life was for a *community.* It was designed by early adopters, like Saint Augustine and Saint Benedict, to hold a community together around shared rhythms of spiritual formation. To center a community on Jesus. And like most things in life, it just plain *works better* in community. We need one another to help us stay on the path and, when we fall, to help us back up.

So: Write up a Rule of Life, even if it's just for yourself. But *if at all possible,* do this in community—with a few friends, with your small group or table community, or, in a dream world, with your entire church.[65]

Will this be harder?

Yes.

Take longer?

I'm sure.

But it will certainly be worth it.

At Bridgetown Church, we spent the last seven years developing our Rule of Life. When we started, most people had never even *heard* the phrase and we had a lot of ground to cover. But before I ever said a *thing* to our church about a Rule of Life, I and a dozen other pastors from various churches had already begun living by a Rule together, falling our way forward. We intuitively knew, we had to *live* it for a while.

Our Rule has plenty of space and flexibility for each person to make it their own; in fact, this is *key* to success. But there's something about knowing you're not alone on the Way. There's something about the joy of keeping Sabbath in *community* and beginning the seventh day with a shared feast that is simply impossible to experience all by yourself. There's something about fasting on Fridays and knowing that we're doing this *together* . . .

In the back you'll find our Rule of Life and more resources, if you're interested in adopting our template or developing your own. We're just here to help. If nothing else, let it spark your imagination.

My point is simple: Do this, yes, but if you can, do it with others, because to follow Jesus is to never be alone . . .

Finally . . .

#9 There is no formation without repetition

Change is all about consistency over time. Formation is slow, cumulative, and at times monotonous work. In the moment, you often don't feel like the practices are "doing" all that much to you. They *are;* it's just slow and subtle. But the philosopher James K. A. Smith said it well: "Micro-rituals have macro significance."[66] They add up over time, like compound interest.

The practices are the spiritual equivalent of Mr. Miyagi and the Karate Kid. In the moment, you just feel like you're waxing Mr. Miyagi's car or pounding nails into the dojo addition, but actually, you're becoming a karate master.

Similarly, in the moment, you just feel like you are reading your Bible before work, going to church on Sunday, or eating another meal with your community on a Thursday night, but actually, you're becoming like the master of all.

But this is a tough pill to swallow in our instant-gratification culture. We're used to getting quick results, and if we don't, we just bail and move on. If we carry this mindset (or, should I say, *when* we carry this mindset) into our formation, we often miss out on the potential for change because we give up far too soon.

There's great joy to be found in repetition, *if* we can learn to be patient and full of delight in the present moment.

No one has ever said this better than G. K. Chesterton:

> Because children have abounding vitality, because they are in spirit fierce and free, therefore they want things

repeated and unchanged. They always say, "Do it again"; and the grown-up person does it again until he is nearly dead. For grown-up people are not strong enough to exult in monotony. But perhaps God is strong enough to exult in monotony. It is possible that God says every morning, "Do it again" to the sun; and every evening, "Do it again" to the moon. It may not be automatic necessity that makes all daisies alike; it may be that God makes every daisy separately, but has never got tired of making them. It may be that he has the eternal appetite of infancy; for we have sinned and grown old, and our Father is younger than we.[67]

So, tomorrow morning when you awake and sit down to pray, *do it again, do it again* . . .

Find your inner monk

One final thing: Following Jesus doesn't work as a hobby. It's not an optional extra to the main point of your life—your career, school, family, sports, or whatever "it" is for you. We simply can't add Jesus to the top of our already overbusy, consumeristic, emotionally unhealthy, hyper-individualistic, digitally distracted, media-saturated, undisciplined modern "life."

It's not that it's bad.

It's that it *won't work,* full stop.

We must come to realize that following Jesus *is* the main point of life. To borrow a term from the world of activism, it's about centering Jesus, making him the dominant voice over your own.

This doesn't mean you need to quit your job and become a monk, but it *does* mean you need to find your "inner monk." The Japanese Canadian pastor Ken Shigematsu wrote, "Every one of us has a monk or nun 'embryo' inside of us."[68] The scholar Greg Peters called it "the monkhood of all believers." [69] Another scholar called it "the monastic impulse."[70]

There's a "monastic impulse" of the Spirit in *all* of us, a part of our hearts that craves quiet prayer, solitude, and contemplation *and* that has a genuine desire (mixed with a tinge of healthy fear) for deep, vulnerable, heart-to-heart relationships with other followers of the Way.

Our inner monk.

If we do not come to desire *some* kind of inner monk (or nun)—long, uninterrupted times of quiet prayer; days of fasting; disciplines of abstinence from our culture's rampant, unbridled pursuit of pleasure, hedonism, and materialism—we simply will not make it very far on the spiritual path.

This, of course, will take a lot of time.

Following Jesus is not convenient, quick, or easy. (Nothing meaningful in life is.)

And there is no way to apprentice Jesus without him interfering in your life, any more than there is a way to apprentice under a master of *any* craft and not have them disrupt how you live.

That's the whole point of learning under a master: you *want* them to disrupt how you live.

And yet: Can you imagine who we could become if we really gave our whole lives over to following Jesus? The kind of life we could enjoy? The kind of community we could become together?

You can do this, and you can do it *right where you are.* In your city, with your job, at your stage of life. Today, you can find your inner monk. One early Christian ascetic gave this advice to "regular" people like you and me, people not living in the distraction-free zone of a monastery:

> Find in the busy city the desert of the monks.[71]

I believe the invitation of Jesus in our day is to live as desert fathers and mothers in the middle of the city. To live with depth and serenity and focus *right in the middle* of the noise and traffic and hurry of the modern world. The both-and of the active, contemplative life.

Will this cost us?

Yes.

We will have to die a thousand deaths, but it will *absolutely* be worth it. With Jesus, you always gain far more than you give up.

In closing, I offer you this from the prologue to *The Rule of St. Benedict,* the Rule that started it all, dating to the sixth century:

> In drawing up its regulations, we hope to set down nothing harsh, nothing burdensome. The good of all concerned, however, may prompt us to a little strict-

ness in order to amend faults and to safeguard love. Do not be daunted immediately by fear and run away from the road that leads to salvation. It is bound to be narrow at the outset. But as we progress in this way of life and in faith, we shall run on the path of God's commandments, our hearts overflowing with the inexpressible delight of love.[72]

What is one small step you can take *this week* in practicing the Way of Jesus?

Or is there something you feel a stirring in your heart to lay down? To leave behind?

What would happen if you were to say *yes* to the impulse of God's Sprit inside you?

Do not fear, and do not run away. The path before you is long and, at times, hard, but it is "overflowing with the inexpressible delight of love."

Practicing the Way—

Take up
your cross

Do you *want* to follow Jesus?

Not everyone does.

Read the Gospels: Tens of thousands of people were drawn to Jesus, but only a few hundred at most became his apprentices. As Mark Scandrette put it, "Practicing the way of Jesus will always be a minority activity."[1]

Jesus' invitation—as I have repeated ad nauseam—was *not* to convert to a new religion called Christianity but to apprentice under him into life in the kingdom of God.

This is the chance of a lifetime, but in the gospel stories, most people said *no* to this invitation.

Many were genuinely drawn to Jesus (how could you *not* be?), but they were not willing to commit to a life of apprenticeship. They made excuses like "First let me go and bury my father," a first-century way of saying, "Let me wait until my parents die so I can get the family inheritance and be independently wealthy; *then* I'll come follow you." Or, "I will follow you, Lord, but first let me go back and say goodbye to my family." Meaning, give me a little more time before I commit.[2]

That's what many of us do: We delay, we seesaw, we make excuses. Like going on a diet or getting in shape or organizing our closet, we procrastinate: "I'll do it *later.*" But later rarely comes.

And what did Jesus say?

Let the dead bury their own dead.

That sounds unkind to our modern ears, but it wasn't; it was just blunt. Jesus was saying, "You can do that, but if you choose that path, it will lead you to death, not life."

You see, Jesus did not beg or manipulate or bully. Coercion is not a fruit of the Spirit. He didn't strong-arm or offer a sales pitch; he just invited. And when people balked or made excuses . . .

He let them walk away.

Can you imagine saying *no* to Jesus' invitation?

I can.

If you live long enough, you will inevitably turn down an invitation you later regret. I have. Thankfully, I can think of only a few opportunities in my life thus far where, in hindsight, I royally missed it. But to this day, when they come to mind, I grieve my decisions.

You have an *invitation* before you to become an apprentice of Jesus.

What will you say?[3]

Surrender

There are a lot of reasons people turn down Jesus' invitation, but as best as I can tell, there's a common denominator in every story: the high bar of entry.

To follow Jesus will require you to leave something behind.

Following Jesus *always* requires you to leave something behind.

For Peter, it was his fishing business. What is it for *you*?

Remember Jesus' words?

> Whoever wants to be my disciple must deny themselves and take up their cross daily and follow me.[4]

For Jesus, step *one* on the spiritual journey is to take up your cross—the ultimate symbol of *death* to self. As Bonhoeffer said, "When Christ calls a man, he bids him come and die."[5] Bonhoeffer, who was later martyred for his faith by the Third Reich, called this "the cost of discipleship."

For the earliest disciples, the cross was a literal one. Most of them were killed, not in spite of their discipleship, but *because* of it. As Jesus warned, "'A servant is not greater than his master.' If they persecuted me, they will persecute you also."[6]

History tells us all twelve apostles were martyred for their faith: James was beheaded in Jerusalem by a paranoid politician.

Peter was crucified upside down. Mark died in Egypt after being dragged through the streets by horses. Luke was hung in Greece. Thomas was stabbed with a spear in India. Matthew was impaled by a sword in Ethiopia. Paul was likely beheaded. "The blood of the martyrs is the seed of the church."[7] Their deaths gave life to millions, including you and me. But they still died.

For most of us in the West, the cross *isn't* literal; it's a metaphor for a settled intention to put to death our self-will, the root of our human problem. To "die to self," as the saying goes. Or as Jaroslav Pelikan, the professor of religious history from Yale, put it, "Christ comes into the world to teach men how to die."[8]

Of course, another word we Christians love for death to self is *surrender.*

Surrender is the foundation of the spiritual life. One of my favorite definitions of *discipleship* is "a lifelong process of deepening surrender to Jesus."[9] This, *this* alone, is *the* ground on which a life of apprenticeship to Jesus is built, as Jesus himself said at the end of his Sermon on the Mount: All others are houses built on sand.

And this is what it means to "love the Lord your God with all your heart." Within the inner chambers of the human heart, love for God and surrender to him are virtually indistinguishable. Jesus himself said, "If you love me, you will keep my commandments."[10]

You see, another, far *less* popular synonym for *surrender* is *obey.*

Within the heart of a true disciple is a settled intention of the will to obey Jesus. As unpopular as the idea of obedience is in the modern era, Jesus *assumes* that his disciples will obey his teachings. Because that's the *very nature* of discipleship: learning "to obey everything [Jesus has] commanded you."[11]

Anything else, though it may use Christian language, is not truly Christian.

An apprentice of Jesus has no other will than the will of God. Your flesh may war against you, and the habits of sin in your "body of death"[12] may sabotage your best intentions. Your "heart may fail"[13] under the emotional weight of life, but your *will* is not in question; your will is devoted to Jesus.

In the value economy of the world, this is utter foolishness—or worse, dangerous. But from the viewpoint of Christian spirituality, the full flowing of the human will, at the zenith of its power, is its capacity to yield itself back to God in loving trust; because it takes more self-mastery to *yield* your will than to *wield* it.

True greatness lies in what the psychologist Gerald May called "willingness," not "willfulness."[14] Or as Thomas Keating beautifully said, "The chief act of the will is not effort but consent."[15] It's to surrender to a power far beyond our own to change us and to a love we can only begin to fathom.

Jesus was the most extraordinary, most free, most powerful human to ever live, yet at the climax of his spiritual prowess, he prayed to the Father, "Not my will, but yours be done."[16]

It's all a long surrender . . .

But this is a *tough* sell in our culture of self-actualization, where we are indoctrinated into the religion of "be true to yourself" and commanded, "If it feels good, do it."

As a result, I find myself caught in the cross currents of desire . . . I want Jesus' life, but I don't want to die.

What about you?

Of course, the great paradox of Christian spirituality is that it's in dying that we live, it's in losing our (false) self that we discover our (true) self, and it's in giving up our desires that our deepest desires are finally sated.

Hence, trust in Jesus is at the very heart of discipleship.

But before you decide whom to trust and which path to follow, let me clarify something *really* important . . .

The cost of (non-)discipleship

We must count the cost not only of following Jesus, but also of *not* following Jesus.

There is a "cost of discipleship," but there is also a cost of *non-*discipleship—that is, it will cost you *not* to apprentice under Jesus.

Surely Jesus intended us to weigh both options. I have no doubt he would encourage you to run a cost-benefit analysis on *both* possible futures: one where you follow the Way and the other where you follow your own path.

When you do the math, you may conclude that, *yes,* following Jesus will cost you—*a lot.* But here's the thing: *Not* following Jesus will cost you even *more.* It will cost you life with God, the very purpose for which you were created. It will cost you access to the inner life of the Trinity, the "peace . . . which transcends all under-standing," and the "joy that is inexpressible and filled with glory."[17] It will cost you freedom from the bondage of sin, healing from the wounding of sin, forgiveness from the guilt and shame of sin, and adoption into the family of God out of the isolation of sin.

People often complain about how hard the spiritual life is. And the honest truth is, yes, it *is.* But what's missing from this diagnosis is that the unspiritual life is even *harder.*

Life is hard, with or without God. But what's *really* hard—nearly unbearable for some—is facing the pain and suffering of life apart from God. So is trying to save yourself rather than be saved. Living in a godless, shepherdless, meaningless universe— that's *really, really* hard.

Ironically, in our attempts to avoid the difficult path of discipleship, we make our life *harder,* not easier. In our pursuit of happiness over obedience, we make our life less and less happy. In our resistance to Jesus' yoke, we end up shouldering the crushing burden of our own unsatisfied desires.

This paradox, which is at the very heart of the gospel itself, is best summarized by Jesus' statement of reality:

> Whoever wants to save their life will lose it, but whoever loses their life for me and for the gospel will save it.[18]

This, of course, is what pretty much *everybody* does—they spend their time, money, and best energies (their "lives") trying to save, protect, guard, enrich, and control their lives in an attempt to be happy and at peace.

And what happens?

They are rarely happy *or* at peace.

We all know people who have rejected Jesus to follow their own paths, only to reach a crisis point (often in midlife or even later), where they say things like "I've lost it all." Or "My life is over." Or "There's no reason to go on living."

No one sets out to be a failure. No one plans to encounter disaster. No one intends to come into old age crippled by missed opportunities and hunched under the staggering weight of regret.

It just happens.

But there is another path—that of apprenticeship to Jesus. The path of giving up all you are to receive all God is.

Jesus told a parable of a man who discovered treasure buried in a field.[19] He then did the most logical thing possible: He went home, sold *all* he had, bought the field, and in return became rich beyond imagination.

That's not heroic or even virtuous; it's just basic arithmetic. What would you do in that situation? What any thinking person would do: Sell everything and, in return, get back far more than you gave up.

This is what following Jesus is like. As the missionary/martyr Jim Elliot put it, "He is no fool who gives what he cannot keep to gain that which he cannot lose."[20]

When Jesus used a financial metaphor for salvation, he did *not* say it was free; he said it would cost your entire life savings, but you would *gain* a thousand times more than you gave up.

That's grace.

So, rather than question, *How much am I willing to surrender to Jesus?* ask yourself honestly, *How joyful, peaceful, and free do I want to be?*

The only true tragedy is to live and not die to self—to forever remain a seed, to never go into the dark humus of the earth and reemerge into the full flowering of your destiny.

As the poet Goethe put it in "The Holy Longing,"

> So long as you haven't experienced this: to die
> and so to grow,
> you are only a troubled guest on the dark earth.[21]

You don't have to be a "troubled guest on the dark earth."

You can be an apprentice of Jesus in the kingdom of God.

Begin again

The Finnish Orthodox writer Tito Colliander told a story about a monk who was once asked, "What do you do there in the monastery?"

The monk replied, "We fall and get up, fall and get up, fall and get up again."[22]

This is a lovely picture of the spiritual journey: falling and getting back up, again and again over the course of a life.

We *will* fail at pretty much everything written in this book. Often. Not just daily but, at least in the beginning, hourly. That doesn't make you a bad apprentice; it just makes you human. The metaphor of walking with God is used all through Scripture; it comes as no surprise, so does its companion metaphor—stumbling. We *will* trip up, ignorantly lose our way, or even blatantly err and wander off the path at times.

It's not a question of *if*, but *when*.

When we stumble, what then?

We begin again.

As Frank Laubach said of his many failures each day to practice the presence of God, "One can begin all over instantly at any moment."[23]

When Benedictine monks enter a monastery, they take a vow to the "conversion of life," which is essentially a lifelong commitment to spiritual formation, to never stop growing. Saint Benedict and many others saw salvation as an ongoing process that *begins* at baptism but does not end until we cross the threshold of death. Or possibly *never* ends. Saint Gregory of Nyssa, who said that "sin happens when we refuse to keep growing," also argued that in heaven "perfection" will be not a fixed state, like in Greek thought, but a kind of endless growth—almost like a Christianized version of evolution and enlightenment, the human creature spiraling ever higher into new realms of possibility in God.[24]

But again, progress is made through death to self, not by climbing some kind of ladder of spiritual success. If there's a ladder, we climb it *down*, not up!

At the risk of a little too much spiritual realism, my own spiritual journey has been marked by more failures than successes. But I strongly suspect I'm not alone.

Hence the need for the conversion of life.

So, in closing, for those of you who want to embark on the journey of a lifetime, let me offer you a few next steps.

1. You must daily hold before your mind and imagination the beauty and possibility of life in the kingdom of God.

Day by day, fill your heart with the wonder of the person, gospel, and life of Jesus. Read and reread the Gospels, pore over each story, turn your mind to him in prayer. Gaze on the Son of God.

2. Once your heart is consumed by a vision of Jesus, you must begin, right where you are. Take one small step, immediately.

Willard was once asked how to become a saint. He answered, "By doing the next right thing."[25]

What's the "next right thing" for *you?*

To step into the waters of baptism? To join a community? To explore a new practice? Or develop a Rule of Life? Or are you simply ready to offer an honest prayer to God now that, although you still have *a lot* of unanswered questions, for the first time, you *want* to want him?

Start *there*.

Jesus has never met anyone anywhere other than where they actually *are*.

3. Take it slow.

Don't try too hard. Relax. "Let life be willed through you."[26] Breathe. Open to God. Start with rest.

Again, it's subtraction, not addition.

There's no hurry at all.

4. *When* you fall (and again, we *all* fall), repent, yes, but don't get sucked into self-recrimination or shame. Fall back on God's mercy. Let him pick you back up.

In this book, I've done my very best to lay out a vision of the wonder of living as an apprentice under Jesus. But all words, certainly my own, fall short of the beauty of such a life.

Now, you must decide: Do you *want* to become an apprentice of Jesus?

Do you want to practice the Way?

If so, you must begin.

As is said in the East, "The journey of a thousand miles begins with one small step."

Just take the first step, then the next, then whatever comes after . . .

Who knows where following the Rabbi will take you?

And when the path is long and hard, when you stumble or lose your way, remember: "fall and get up, fall and get up, fall and get up."

And begin again.

Practicing the Way—

Extras

The Practicing the Way Course is an eight-week introduction to spiritual formation, designed to be run in your church or small group. If you participate in the course, you and your community will walk away with:

- A Spiritual Health Reflection

- An understanding of what it means to apprentice under Jesus and a working grasp of spiritual formation

- A formation audit of your current life and a plan for intentional counter-formation

- Embodied training in spiritual practices, including Sabbath, solitude, prayer, Scripture, and more

- A Rule of Life

- A plan for table-based community

- Personalized next steps in your apprenticeship to Jesus

To run the course, visit practicingtheway.org/courses.

A Rule of Life from Practicing the Way

1. A community of rest in a culture of hurry and exhaustion, through the practice of *Sabbath*.

2. A community of peace and quiet in a culture of anxiety and noise, through the practice of *solitude*.

3. A community of communion with God in a culture of distraction and escapism, through the practice of *prayer*.

4. A community of love and depth in a culture of individualism and superficiality, through the practice of *community*.

5. A community of courageous fidelity to orthodoxy in a culture of ideological compromise, through the practice of *Scripture*.

6. A community of holiness in a culture of indulgence and immorality, through the practice of *fasting*.

7. A community of contentment in a culture of consumerism, through the practice of *generosity*.

8. A community of justice, mercy, and reconciliation in a culture of injustice and division, through the practice of *service*.

9. A community of hospitality in a culture of hostility, through the practice of *witness*.

The nine practices

Practices	Sabbath	Prayer	Fasting
Daily		*Prayer rhythm*	
Weekly	*Sabbath day to stop, rest, delight, and worship*		*Fast until sundown*
Monthly or Seasonally			

Practices	Solitude	Scripture	Community
Daily	*A time in silence to begin or end the day*	*Reading Scripture*	
Weekly			*A meal together and worship on Sunday*
Monthly or Seasonally			

The nine practices

Practices	Generosity	Service	Witness
Daily			
Weekly			
Monthly or Seasonally	*Giving away 10 percent of your income, with special attention to the church and the poor*	*An act of service to the poor with the aim of kinship*	*An act of hospitality and regularly praying for one person in your life who doesn't know Jesus*

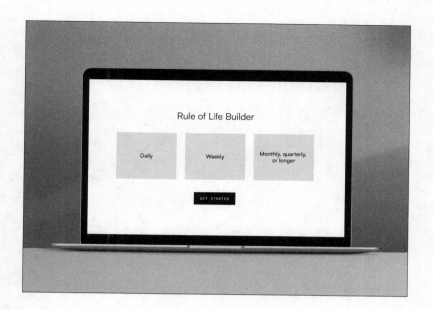

The Rule of Life Builder

There's no one-size-fits-all approach to spiritual formation. A Rule of Life can serve as an anchor point to hold a community together around Jesus, but each member must customize the Rule to fit the contours of their life. And a Rule isn't meant to be static, but dynamic, as your life changes with the seasons and stages.

To that end, we've created a free digital tool for you to design your own Rule of Life. Begin now by going to practicingtheway.org/ruleoflifebuilder.

Gratitude

The longer I live, the more the best summary of my heart simply becomes *thank you.*

So many people invested their time, perspiration, wisdom, and love into this project. My heart is chock full of gratitude. Thank you to . . .

- Bridgetown Church. This book was born out of our journey together, and I will carry you in my heart forever: I love you.

- My literary agent, Mike Salisbury, for going *far* beyond what is normal; my Yoda. And to all the team at Yates & Yates—Matt, Curtis, and Sealy Yates, and Kristina Troup.

- The entire team at Practicing the Way—we have a *team* now, woohoo!—but especially Cameron Doolittle for running *everything* so I can focus on writing; Sydney Bolinger for being a *boss* and being so very kind; Lisa Oliver for the patient dedication to the craft; Evan Oliver for plane flights, camera rentals, and warm smiles; and most of all, Deanna Gilday for twelve years of partnership filled with more joy and kindness than most people experience in a lifetime.

- The RWP. Dude, love ya. Next one?

- Everyone at Penguin Random House and WaterBrook—Tina Constable, Laura Barker, Douglas

Mann, Campbell Wharton, Brett Benson, and all the team. You have been so very good to me.

- Paul Pastor, Drew Dixon, Laura Wright, Tracey Moore, and all those who worked so tirelessly to edit this book into its final state; thank you for your patience with my indecision, perfectionism, and slow email responses . . .

- All my beta readers—you know who you are—but especially to Gerry Breshears; I still can't believe you! And Sam Aker (ninja!) for both your literary analysis and help with the final edits.

- Special thanks to Jason Ballard, Tyler Staton, Bethany Allen, and Gavin Bennet for being thought partners on all things Practicing the Way and to Gordie Cochran, Tim Choy, and the entire crew at Colours and Shapes for turning this vision into a reality.

- My kids—Jude, Moses, and Sunday—for all the love and patience with your introverted dad, and my lovely wife, T, for your unflagging encouragement through all the ups and downs of the last few years.

Finally, it feels clumsy and wrong to tag God onto a list of gratitudes, but . . . God of Triune Love, I offer the inspired words of the heavenly community back to you in love:

> You are worthy, our Lord and God,
>> to receive glory and honor and power,
> for you created all things,
>> and by your will they were created
>> and have their being.[1]

Notes

Dust

Epigraph: "Let your house be a meeting place for the rabbis, and cover yourself in the dust of their feet, and drink in their words thirstily" is a statement attributed to Yose ben Yoezer, a rabbi in the second century B.C. Some scholars think "cover yourself in the dust" referred to the dirt that would inevitably get on a disciple's clothes from sitting at a teacher's feet for hours on end; others argue that it referred to following the rabbi over dusty roads for days at a time, getting as close as one could to not miss a word. Either way, it was a blessing of proximity, of being so close to the rabbi that the disciple got dusty. See Ann Spangler and Lois Tverberg, *Sitting at the Feet of Rabbi Jesus: How the Jewishness of Jesus Can Transform Your Faith* (Grand Rapids, Mich.: Zondervan, 2018), 18–19.

1. Robert N. Bellah et al., *Habits of the Heart: Individualism and Commitment in American Life, with a New Preface* (Berkeley: University of California Press, 2008).

2. John Donne, *Devotions upon Emergent Occasions and Death's Duel* (New York: Vintage, 1999), 103.

3. Tish is also one of the best contemporary writers on formation. This is from her book *Prayer in the Night: For Those Who Work or Watch or Weep* (Downers Grove, Ill.: InterVarsity, 2021), 82 (italics added).

4. See *The Rise and Triumph of the Modern Self: Cultural Amnesia, Expressive Individualism, and the Road to Sexual Revolution* by Carl R. Trueman (Wheaton, Ill.: Crossway, 2020), which I think is one of the most important Christian books written in the last decade.

5. Jaron Lanier, *Ten Arguments for Deleting Your Social Media Accounts Right Now* (London: Vintage, 2019), 6. Read this book! "Right now."

6. For this line, I'm indebted to the fine work of Chris Cruz, who originally said, "If we're not intentionally choosing to be discipled by Jesus, we're being unintentionally discipled by the world." *The Practice of Being with Jesus* (Redding, Calif.: Chris Cruz, 2020), 5.

7. When people say (as I often hear in L.A.), "I don't believe in God; I believe in science," they are letting it slip that they believe in something, just not in God. Despite the popular shtick that secular people just believe in the "cold, hard facts," not the "opinions and feelings" of religion, in reality they have chosen to put their trust in another person's *interpretation* of the data points of science rather than in a religion or teacher like Jesus (or other intelligent scientific thinkers who very much believe in God). The difference isn't between believing in facts and believing in feelings; it's between choosing to put your or one's faith in a secular interpretation of science and choosing to trust in a theistic interpretation. Rant over.

8. John 6v68.

9. See Luke 14v27–30, ESV.

10. 1 Timothy 6v19.

11. Matthew 4v19.

Apprentice to Jesus

1. Mark 1v17.

2. Mark 1v18.

3. *Merriam-Webster,* s.v. "rabbi," www.merriam-webster.com /dictionary/rabbi#word-history.

4. Fun fact: The word translated "carpenter" in the Gospels is *tekton,* and it could also mean "any craftsman or workman." Henry George Liddell and Robert Scott, comps., *A Greek-English Lexicon,* 9th ed., with rev. supplement (Oxford: Clarendon Press, 1996), 1769. Galilee had very few trees. Homes were made out of stone, and most people sat on the floor to eat and relax, not at tables or in chairs. Very few things were made out of wood (besides doors and a few tools). So, as much as people love to imagine Jesus with a bow lathe making Mary a beautiful rocking chair, it's more likely he was a stonemason.

5. Ann Spangler and Lois Tverberg, *Sitting at the Feet of Rabbi Jesus: How the Jewishness of Jesus Can Transform Your Faith* (Grand Rapids, Mich.: Zondervan, 2018), 31–32.

6. Here is a great, short explanation of the title *rabbi* in the first century: https://ourrabbijesus .com/articles/can-we-call-jesus -rabbi.

7. As Gerald L. Sittser said, "Rabbis would gather a circle of disciples and teach them how to interpret and obey the law of Moses. They gained their authority by attending a rabbinic school and learning from a recognized rabbi, who would always teach from within the framework of a particular rabbinic tradition. Jesus was unusual because he did not follow that conventional pathway. He never attended a school, never studied under an established rabbi, and never taught his followers a rabbinic tradition. He never once even quoted a rabbi. If anything, he accused rabbis of failing to teach the real meaning of the law of Moses." *Resilient Faith: How the Early Christian "Third Way" Changed the World* (Grand Rapids, Mich.: Brazos, 2019), 29.

8. Matthew 22v33; Mark 9v15.

9. Luke 4v22.

10. Mark 1v22.

11. Matthew 13v54; John 7v46.

12. Dallas Willard, *The Great Omission: Reclaiming Jesus's Essential Teachings on Discipleship* (New York: HarperOne, 2014), 19.

13. Spangler and Tverberg, *Sitting at the Feet of Rabbi Jesus,* 38. I keep referencing this because it's a phenomenal book on the Jewish background of the four Gospels.

14. John 10v33. Only modern skeptics argue that Jesus "never claimed to be God." His original listeners had the exact opposite interpretation. It's just lost in translation to our modern ears because Jesus didn't lay it out in a Western-style academic essay; instead, it's in parable, allusion, and story that he constantly put himself—in word and deed—in the place where only God is. Or he said things like "Anyone who has seen me has seen the Father" (John 14v9).

15. The recommended ages for study are found in the Mishnah, Pirkei Avot 5:21 (www.sefaria.org /Pirkei_Avot.5.21?lang=bi). More information on the three levels of education can be found in *Educational Ideals in the Ancient World* by William Barclay (n.p.: Creative Media Partners, 2021).

16. Rob Bell, "Covered in the Dust of Your Rabbi," sermon, YouTube video, 23:08, www.youtube.com /watch?v=aCtrsJ6nSio.

17. Bell, "Covered in the Dust of Your Rabbi," 17:57.

18. Mark 3v14.

19. Luke 6v40. For clarity, I've used the words *apprentice* and *rabbi* in place of the NIV's *student* and *teacher*.

20. Ray Vander Laan, "Rabbi and Talmidim," That the World May Know. Ray's stuff is just gold.

21. Spangler and Tverberg, *Sitting at the Feet of Rabbi Jesus,* 58.

22. Willard, *The Great Omission,* 6.

23. *Strong's Definitions,* s.v. "*talmid,*" Blue Letter Bible, www.bluabletter bible.org/lexicon/h8527/kjv/wlc/0-1.

24. In Greek, the language of the New Testament, the primary word used is *mathētēs.* The verb *mathēteuō* is used in a few verses but is translated as "to be a disciple" or "to make disciples" (*Blue Letter Bible,* s.v. "*mathēteuō,*" www.bluabletter bible.org/lexicon/g3100/esv/mgnt/0-1)—so *disciple* is still used as a noun. Both Matthew 28v19 and Acts 14v21 use this term in connection to the gospel. But even then, I would interpret it to refer to preaching the gospel in such a way that people become apprentices of Jesus, not just "converts" to a religious view.

25. Or, if you're in the role of an older, wiser mentor, it's something you do to a younger adherent of the Way. You "disciple" them.

26. This line is based on a lovely quote from Dallas Willard in *The Great Omission:* "The New Testament is a book about disciples, by disciples, and for disciples of Jesus Christ," page 3.

27. John Ortberg, *Eternity Is Now in Session: A Radical Rediscovery of What Jesus Really Taught About Salvation, Eternity, and Getting to the Good Place* (Carol Stream, Ill.: Tyndale, 2018), 49.

28. Michael Burkhimer, *Lincoln's Christianity* (Yardley, Pa.: Westholme, 2007), xi.

29. For those of you reading from outside the US, I love you and apologize for the US-centric stats about to come your way.

30. Gregory A. Smith, "About Three in Ten US Adults Are Now Religiously Unaffiliated," Pew Research Center, December 14, 2021, www.pewresearch.org/religion/2021/12/14/about-three-in-ten-u-s-adults-are-now-religiously-unaffiliated.

31. "American Worldview Inventory 2023," Barna, February 28, 2023, www.arizonachristian.edu/wp-content/uploads/2023/02/CRC_AWVI2023_Release1.pdf.

32. "Maximus the Confessor: Two Hundred Texts on Theology and the Incarnate Dispensation of the Son of God," Orthodox Church Fathers,

https://orthodoxchurchfathers
.com/fathers/philokalia/maximus
-the-confessor-two-hundred-texts
-on-theology-and-the-incarnate
-dispensati.html.

33. Case in point: Most churches
have a statement of faith that they
often require members to sign, but
few have a statement of ethics that
requires members to follow the
Sermon on the Mount or a Rule of
Life that requires them to organize
their days around prayer in any
concrete way.

34. Remember, Jesus had only
twelve apostles but scores of followers.

35. Willard, *The Great Omission,* xv.

36. David Kinnaman and Mark
Matlock, *Faith for Exiles: 5 Ways for a
New Generation to Follow Jesus in Dig-
ital Babylon* (Grand Rapids, Mich.:
Baker, 2019), 32. That stat is for
America, but they studied twenty-
six countries. The results are simi-
lar in other Western contexts like
the UK or Australia but higher in
Asian and African countries.

37. Do I have your attention now?

38. For a more in-depth, nuanced
look at this, you're welcome to listen to a teaching series I did called
Preaching the Gospel, at www

.practicingtheway.org/practices
/preaching-the-gospel. I'd recommend the teaching "The Four
American Gospels."

39. Actually, this example is from
my seminary professor, Dr. Gerry
Breshears. He calls it "the John 3:16
gospel."

40. Ortberg, *Eternity Is Now in Session,* Kindle.

41. Matthew 7v21.

42. "What the Bible Says About
Hamartia," *Forerunner Commentary,*
Bible Tools, www.bibletools.org
/index.cfm/fuseaction/topical
.show/RTD/cgg/ID/1677
/Hamartia.htm.

43. Luke 19v10.

44. Mark 1v15.

45. Matthew 11v25.

46. Willard, *The Great Omission,* 61.

47. Matthew 7v26–27.

48. I'm pulling this line and idea
straight from John Ortberg, *Eternity
Is Now in Session,* 8.

49. Bishop Kallistos Ware, *The
Orthodox Way,* rev. ed. (Crestwood,
N.Y.: St. Vladimir's Seminary, 1995),
7–8. When I read this absolutely
wonderful book, it felt like coming
home.

50. John 14v6.

51. Eugene H. Peterson, *The Jesus*

Way (Grand Rapids, Mich.: Eerdmans, 2007).

52. Matthew 7v13–14.

53. John 10v10.

54. Psalm 23v5.

55. Mark 8v34.

56. For those of you who have, was it worth it?

57. *"The Count of Monte Cristo* (2002): Quotes," Internet Movie Database, www.imdb.com/title/tt0245844 /quotes/?ref_=tt_trv_qu.

Goal #1: Be with Jesus

1. John 1v39, ESV.

2. "Sitting at his feet" was an idiom for being a disciple of a rabbi. We have no records of any rabbis except Jesus taking on female disciples.

3. Mark 3v13–14.

4. Luke 9v2.

5. John 14v16.

6. HELPS Word-studies, s.v., *"allos,"* Bible Hub, https://biblehub.com /greek/243.htm.

7. *Strong's Concordance,* s.v., *"paraklētos,"* Bible Hub, https:// biblehub.com/greek/3875.htm.

8. John 14v26.

9. John 15v4, ESV.

10. "What Does It Mean to Abide?" Precept Austin, August 6, 2022, www.preceptaustin.org/what -does-it-mean-to-abide.

11. *Pleeeease* read *Stolen Focus* by Johann Hari or *Ten Arguments for Deleting Your Social Media Accounts Right Now* by Jaron Lanier.

12. From Galatians 5v22–23— what a passage!

13. 1 Timothy 6v19; 1 Thessalonians 5:17, ESV.

14. Chel Avery, "Traditional Quaker Worship," Quaker Information Center, May 26, 2011, https:// quakerinfo.org/quakerism /worship.

15. Jean-Pierre de Caussade, *The Sacrament of the Present Moment,* trans. Kitty Muggeridge (San Francisco: HarperSanFrancisco, 1989).

16. A. W. Tozer, *The Pursuit of God: The Human Thirst for the Divine* (Chicago: Moody, 2015), chaps. 3, 4.

17. Dallas Willard, "An Invitation to a 'With-God Life' in Jesus," Dallas Willard Ministries, YouTube video, www.youtube.com/watch?v =HN1K43YePCc.

18. Brother Lawrence, *The Practice of the Presence of God; with the Maxims of Brother Lawrence* (Topeka, Kans.: Christ the King Library, 2017).

19. The first quote here is John Ortberg's summary of Mihaly Csikszentmihalyi; please see www.you

tube.com/watch?v=TPWUy81
YHiA. The second quote is Csik-
szentmihalyi himself, *Flow: The Psy-
chology of Optimal Experience* (New
York: Harper Perennial Modern
Classics, 2008), chap. 2.

20. Brother Lawrence, *Practice of
the Presence of God,* 6.

21. Thomas R. Kelly, *A Testament of
Devotion* (San Francisco: Harper-
SanFrancisco, 1992), 15.

22. A phrase from the sci-fi writer
Cory Doctorow in "Writing in the
Age of Distraction," *Locus Magazine,*
January 2009, www.locusmag.com
/Features/2009/01/cory
-doctorow-writing-in-age-of.html.

23. Dallas Willard, *The Great Omis-
sion: Reclaiming Jesus's Essential
Teachings on Discipleship* (New York:
HarperOne, 2014), 125.

24. Psalm 16v8, ESV.

25. Colossians 3v2.

26. Hwee Hwee Tan, "In Search of
the Lotus Land," *Quarterly Literary
Review Singapore* 1 no. 1 (October 2001), www.qlrs.com/essay
.asp?id=140.

27. Thank you, Rousseau.

28. Tozer, *Pursuit of God,* chap. 7.

29. Frank C. Laubach, *Letters by a
Modern Mystic* (London: Society for
Promoting Christian Knowledge,
2011), 75 (italics added).

30. Marjorie J. Thompson, *Soul
Feast: An Invitation to the Christian
Spiritual Life,* newly rev. ed. (Louis-
ville: Westminster John Knox,
2014), 44.

31. David L. Fleming, *What Is Ignatian Spirituality?* (Chicago: Loyola
Press, 2008), 8.

32. From *On Union With God* and
Life of Theoria in the fifth volume of
The Philokalia. If you want to go
deep, read *The Philokalia.* It's currently changing my life.

33. 2 Corinthians 3v18.

34. Psalm 27v4.

35. Hopefully coming soon . . .

36. Ephesians 3v16–19.

37. The word used by Paul is
ginōskō, and it means a relational
knowing, as in I "know" my wife T.
Thayer's Greek Lexicon, s.v. *"ginōskō,"*
Blue Letter Bible, www.bluenetter
bible.org/lexicon/g1097/niv
/mgnt/0-1.

38. David G. Benner, *Surrender to
Love: Discovering the Heart of Chris-
tian Spirituality* (Downers Grove,
Ill.: InterVarsity, 2003), 92.

39. "Paying Attention: The
Attention Economy," *Berkeley
Economic Review,* March 31, 2020,
https://econreview.berkeley.edu
/paying-attention-the-attention
-economy.

40. Simone Weil, *Gravity and Grace,* trans. Arthur Wills (New York: G. P. Putnam's Sons, 1952), 170.

41. Douglas V. Steere, *Together in Solitude* (New York: Crossroad, 1982), 25, quoted in Arthur Boers, *Living into Focus: Choosing What Matters in an Age of Distractions* (Grand Rapids, Mich.: Brazos, 2012), 48.

42. Richard Plass and James Cofield, *The Relational Soul: Moving from False Self to Deep Connection* (Downers Grove, Ill.: IVP Books, 2014), 143.

43. This is why Christian mystics have long said sexual union in marriage is the ultimate example of our union with God; it starts with words but goes far beyond that into the intermingling of souls. For an excellent overview of this stream of rich Christian thought, read *Fill These Hearts: God, Sex, and the Universal Longing* by Christopher West (New York: Image, 2012).

44. Karl Rahner, *Theological Investigations,* vol. XX, *Concern for the Church,* trans. Edward Quinn (New York: Crossroad, 1981), 149.

45. The theological term for this is *incorporation,* and scholars argue it's the dominant theme of Paul's writings. It's used more than seventy times in his letters.

46. Colossians 3v3.

47. Colossians 1v27.

48. Single origin, preferably Central American, from Coava—made in a Chemex, 'cause OBV.

49. Henri Nouwen, "From Solitude to Community to Ministry," *Leadership* 16 (Spring 1995), www .christianitytoday.com/pastors /1995/spring/5l280.html.

50. Genesis 15v1, NKJV.

51. John 15v15, ESV.

52. Thomas à Kempis, *The Imitation of Christ,* trans. Rev. R. Challoner (Dublin: McGlashan and Gill, 1873), 113, www.google.com /books/edition/The_Imitation _of_Christ/NKPnvCS9j1EC.

53. Luke 10v39.

54. 1 Timothy 6v19.

55. Matthew 6v6, NKJV.

56. Bible Hub, s.v. "*tameion,*" https://biblehub.com/ greek/5009.htm.

57. Mark 1v35.

58. Blue Letter Bible, s.v. "*erēmos,*" www.blueletterbible.org/lexicon /g2048/niv/mgnt/0-1.

59. Luke 5v16.

60. Luke 22v39.

61. Luke 22v39, AMP.

62. John 18v2.

63. Henri J. M. Nouwen, *Making All Things New: An Invitation to the Spiri-*

tual Life (San Francisco: HarperSan-Francisco, 1981), 69.

64. Henri J. M. Nouwen, *Beloved: Henri Nouwen in Conversation,* with Philip Roderick (Grand Rapids, Mich.: William B. Eerdmans, 2007), 30–31.

65. To put all my cards on the table, I don't think it's unrealistic for most people. The "average" person spends over two hours a day on social media and around three hours a day watching TV. "Average Daily Time Spent on Social Media (Latest 2023 Data)," Broadband Search, www.broadbandsearch.net /blog/average-daily-time-on-social -media; Rebecca Lake, "Television Statistics: 23 Mind-Numbing Facts to Watch," CreditDonkey, February 26, 2023, www.creditdonkey.com /television-statistics.html. And even for those who honestly don't have an hour, most people can rearrange their lives to make space for time alone with God, should they so choose. For young parents and those with demanding, early-start jobs, it may require great creativity, but for most, it can be done.

66. Yep. Tyler is the real deal.

67. That said, thank you, James Clear, for this incredibly helpful idea. I highly recommend his book *Atomic Habits.*

68. See my previous book *The Ruthless Elimination of Hurry* where I tell this story (18–19).

69. A short word to pastors: As a result of our well-meaning desires to see our churches flourish, people often experience our leadership as an attempt to add things into their already overbusy lives. Sunday becomes less like a Sabbath and more like a religious workday. What if we were to see ourselves as spiritual guides to help people live a slower life with Jesus? What if we were to structure Sundays as a "habit" designed to unhurry our community, quiet their minds and bodies, and help them cultivate a deeper life of abiding? Henry Nouwen once said this to pastors: "Our task is the opposite of distraction. Our task is to help people concentrate on the real but often hidden event of God's active presence in their lives. Hence, the question that must guide all organizing activity in a parish is not how to keep people busy, but how to keep them from being so busy that they can no longer hear the voice of God who speaks in silence." *The Way of the Heart: Desert Spirituality and Contemporary Ministry* (San

Francisco: HarperSanFrancisco, 1991), 63.

70. Rich Villodas, *The Deeply Formed Life: Five Transformative Values to Root Us in the Way of Jesus* (Colorado Springs: WaterBrook, 2020), 3–5.

71. As A. W. Tozer put it, "It is well that we accept the hard truth now: *the man who would know God must give time to Him.* He must count no time wasted which is spent in the cultivation of His acquaintance. He must give himself to meditation and prayer hours on end. So did the saints of old, the glorious company of the apostles, the goodly fellowship of the prophets and the believing members of the holy church in all generations. And so must we if we would follow in their train." *God's Pursuit of Man* (Chicago: Moody, 2015), 20–21.

72. To do this, run the Practicing the Way course at www.practicing theway.org.

73. Ronald Rolheiser, *The Holy Longing: The Search for a Christian Spirituality* (New York: Doubleday, 1999), 9.

74. John 1v39, NLT.

Goal #2: Become like him

1. But . . . it almost was. After hearing me say on a podcast a version of what I'm about to share about monks and skulls, a good friend of mine who does work in Mexico called me. "I know a guy who can get you a real skull," he said. Apparently, there's a certain booth at a Mexico City market where you can ask for a "guy who knows a guy" kind of thing. I genuinely thought about it, but it quickly became an ethical quagmire. So instead, I opted for a ceramic mold off Etsy.

2. Benedict, *The Rule of St. Benedict in English,* ed. Timothy Fry (Collegeville, Minn.: Liturgical Press, 2019), chap. 4.

3. From the title of his book. Neil Postman, *Amusing Ourselves to Death: Public Discourse in the Age of Show Business* (New York: Penguin, 2006).

4. Ronald Rolheiser, *The Holy Longing: The Search for a Christian Spirituality* (New York: Image, 2019).

5. David Brooks, *The Road to Character* (New York: Random House, 2015), xi.

6. Luke 6v40; see also Matthew 10v24. (Again, I've substituted *apprentice* and *rabbi* for *student* and *teacher* here.)

7. For the record, I do not mean this statement philosophically, as in personhood theory (the idea that both abortion and euthanasia are based on), which says that a human has to reach a certain level of development to qualify as a person deserving of human rights. (See Nancy Pearcey's phenomenal book *Love Thy Body*.) I mean it rhetorically: You're becoming a type of soul, luminous in beauty or defaced by sin.

8. This is my paraphrase of M. Robert Mulholland Jr. in *Invitation to a Journey: A Road Map for Spiritual Formation,* expanded ed. (Downers Grove, Ill.: IVP Books, 2016).

9. Mulholland, *Invitation to a Journey,* 28.

10. His main work on hell was *The Great Divorce,* but these two phrases are from C. S. Lewis, *The Weight of Glory* (New York: HarperCollins, 2001), 46.

11. Dallas Willard, *The Great Omission: Reclaiming Jesus's Essential Teachings on Discipleship* (New York: HarperOne, 2014).

12. A technically true but terrible saying.

13. John 10v11–16; Jeremiah 18v6; Isaiah 42v14; 49v15.

14. At some level, we're all addicts. The question is, to what?

15. Luke 6v28.

16. 1 John 4v8.

17. Augustine, *The Trinity (De Trinitate),* trans. Edmund Hill, ed. John E. Rotelle (Hyde Park, N.Y.: New City, 2015).

18. John 15v13.

19. 1 John 3v16.

20. Mulholland, *Invitation to a Journey,* 16. This is one of my all-time favorite books on formation; I can't recommend it enough.

21. Colossians 1v27.

22. You must read this book! Darrell W. Johnson, *Experiencing the Trinity: Living in the Relationship at the Centre of the Universe* (Vancouver, BC: Canadian Church Leaders Network, 2021), 53.

23. John 17v20–21, 23.

24. Matthew 7v14.

25. Cheesy analogy: Growth will happen to all children; they will all get bigger. But turning your body into an Arnold Schwarzenegger will not "just happen." That is the result of serious training (and Greek-god genetics). Same with becoming like Jesus.

26. Janet O. Hagberg and Robert A. Guelich, *The Critical Journey: Stages in the Life of Faith,* 2nd ed. (Salem, Wis.: Sheffield, 2005), 7.

27. Hagberg and Guelich, *Critical Journey,* chap. 7. I often think of Jesus' parable of the sower. I highly doubt Jesus was giving us a statistical average; still, only one-quarter of people bear any fruit at all long term, and only one-third of that group (8 percent) bear maximum fruit.

28. A few reasons: (1) People hit "the Wall" (a painful experience that you can't go around—the only way out is through). Hagberg and Guelich, *Critical Journey,* chap. 7. (2) Most discipleship models don't offer anything beyond stages two and three. (3) We live in a first-half-of-life culture that often intentionally tries to keep people immature.

29. Lisa Bodell, "New Year's Resolutions Fail. Do This Instead," *Forbes,* December 19, 2022, www .forbes.com/sites/lisabodell/2022 /12/19/new-years-resolutions -fail-do-this-instead/?sh=1b5c2cc 57c8b.

30. Leslie Jamison, *The Recovering: Intoxication and Its Aftermath* (New York: Back Bay Books, 2018), 304.

31. 2 Timothy 3v16.

32. I heard it this way in a small, private teaching. He says it similarly, "We can't think our way to holiness," in this source: James K. A. Smith, *You Are What You Love: The Spiritual Power of Habit* (Grand Rapids, Mich.: Brazos, 2016), 5.

33. Thanks to Cameron Doolittle for this great analogy.

34. Francis Spufford, *Unapologetic: Why, Despite Everything, Christianity Can Still Make Surprising Emotional Sense* (New York: HarperOne, 2013), 27–28.

35. Bishop Kallistos Ware, *The Orthodox Way,* rev. ed. (Crestwood, N.Y.: St. Vladimir's Seminary, 1995), 62.

36. Romans 3v26, ESV. This means he's both a just judge and the one who died to justify us.

37. This list was compiled from the teaching of Dr. Gerry Breshears, who first introduced me to the idea of atonement theories being like a multifaceted diamond. You can access his teaching on the Atonement in Lesson 21, "Life of Jesus," of this theology course from Biblical Training: www.biblicaltraining.org /learn/academy/th104-a-guide -to-christian-theology.

38. Dan B. Allender, *Sabbath: The Ancient Practices* (Nashville, Tenn.: Thomas Nelson, 2009), 7.

39. Luke 5v31–32.

40. Ignatius, "VII. Beware of False Teachers," in *The Epistle of Ignatius* to the Ephesians: Shorter and Longer Versions, in Ante-Nicene Fathers, vol. 1, The Apostolic Fathers, Justin Martyr, Irenaeus, ed. Alexander Roberts and James Donaldson, Christian Classics Ethereal Library, https://ccel.org/ccel/schaff/anf01/anf01.v.ii.vii.html.

41. Thayer's Greek Lexicon, s.v. "sōzō," Blue Letter Bible, www.blueletter bible.org/lexicon/g4982/esv /mgnt/0-1.

42. Luke 8v48.

43. As Dallas Willard said, "Any successful plan for spiritual formation . . . will in fact be significantly similar to the Alcoholics Anonymous program." Renovation of the Heart: Putting on the Character of Christ, 20th anniv. ed. (Colorado Springs: NavPress, 2021), 83.

44. James Baldwin, "As Much Truth as One Can Bear," New York Times, January 14, 1962.

45. Matthew 11v30, MSG.

46. Aaron Lewendon, "Eden Q&A with Pete Hughes about All Things New," February 4, 2020, www.eden .co.uk/blog/eden-q-a-with-pete -hughes-about-all-things-new -p1783328.

47. Charles Duhigg, The Power of Habit: Why We Do What We Do in Life and Business (New York: Random House, 2023).

48. Pete Scazzero (@petescazzero), Twitter, June 30, 2017, https:// twitter.com/petescazzero/status /880864831808700416?lang=en.

49. Flannery O'Connor, The Habit of Being, ed. Sally Fitzgerald (New York: Vintage, 1980), 229.

50. Tish Harrison Warren, Liturgy of the Ordinary: Sacred Practices in Everyday Life (Downers Grove, Ill.: IVP Books, 2016), 31.

51. A. W. Tozer, The Knowledge of the Holy (n.p.: Fig, 2012), 4, www .amazon.com/Knowledge-Holy-W -Tozer/dp/1626309906.

52. Matthew 5v19.

53. Matthew 7v24.

54. My favorite book on community. Joseph H. Hellerman, When the Church Was a Family: Recapturing Jesus' Vision for Authentic Christian Community (Nashville, Tenn.: B & H Academic, 2009), 1.

55. He went on to write, "God hates this wishful dreaming because it makes the dreamer proud and pretentious. Those who dream of this idealized community demand that it be fulfilled by God, by others, and by themselves. They enter the community of Christians with their demands, set up their own law, and judge one another and even God accordingly." Dietrich Bonhoeffer, *Life Together and Prayerbook of the Bible,* ed. Geffrey B. Kelly, trans. Daniel W. Bloesch and James H. Burtness (Minneapolis: Fortress, 2005), 36.

56. Revelation 7v10.

57. Eugene H. Peterson, *A Long Obedience in the Same Direction: Discipleship in an Instant Society* (Downers Grove, Ill.: InterVarsity, 2021).

58. Madeline Joung, "Millennial Life: Eat, Sleep, Work, Screens," Voice of America, November 18, 2020, www.voanews.com/a /student-union_millennial-life-eat -sleep-work-screens/6198558 .html.

59. James 1v2–4.

60. Romans 5v3–4.

61. 1 Peter 1v6–7.

62. For a great summary of this interpretation, I'd recommend *Them: Why We Hate Each Other—and How to Heal* by Ben Sasse (New York: St. Martin's, 2018).

63. Jacques Ellul, *The Technological Society* (New York: Vintage, 1964).

64. John 16v21.

Goal #3: Do as he did

1. My paraphrase of Matthew 28v19. The NIV has "of all nations," but the word is *ethnos* in Greek and is closer to "ethnic groups" than "nation-states."

2. Mishnah, Pirkei Avot 1:1.

3. Mark 1v17, ESV.

4. Warren Wiersbe, *The Wiersbe Bible Commentary: New Testament* (Colorado Springs: David C Cook, 2007), 92.

5. Patrick O'Connell, "The 5 Steps of Leadership Development," Aspen Group, October 29, 2020, www .aspengroup.com/blog/five-steps -of-leadership-development.

6. Luke 10v37.

7. 1 John 2v5–6.

8. This is another translation of the Greek word translated "firstfruits" in 1 Corinthians 15v20–26.

9. The classic example is Thomas Jefferson's Bible, where he literally cut out all the miracle stories and anything that didn't align with his deistic worldview.

10. To which skeptics replied, "Who cares? The Bible is just a collection of human writings."

11. Luke 4v14, 18–19.

12. Arthur Michael Ramsey, *God,*

Christ and the World: A Study in Contemporary Theology (Eugene, Ore.: Wipf and Stock, 2012), 37.

13. John 14v12.

14. Some argue he means quantity, not quality. Now that there are millions of followers of Jesus around the world, they can carry his work of healing and deliverance to more people than he ever could alone. That's a leading interpretation.

15. Henri Nouwen, "From Solitude to Community to Ministry," *Leadership* 16 (Spring 1995), www.christianitytoday.com /pastors/1995/spring/5l280.html.

16. Of course, most of this is due to the Christian-disciple bifurcation in Western culture, but not all. The changing moral calculus around sexuality and gender has sparked an increased venom toward even the most loving and thoughtful of Jesus' apprentices.

17. Luke 19v7.

18. Mary Douglas, *Implicit Meanings: Selected Essays in Anthropology* (London: Routledge, 2010).

19. Give me Chipotle anytime . . .

20. Robert J. Karris, *Luke: Artist and Theologian* (Eugene, Ore.: Wipf and Stock, 2008), 47.

21. Luke 7v34.

22. Robert J. Karris, *Eating Your Way Through Luke's Gospel* (Collegeville, Minn.: Liturgical, 2006), 14.

23. Tim Chester, *A Meal with Jesus: Discovering Grace, Community, and Mission Around the Table* (Seoul: IVP, 2013), introduction.

24. Luke 19v10.

25. Luke 7v34.

26. Chester, *Meal with Jesus,* introduction.

27. "Romans 12:10–13 Commentary," Precept Austin, February 21, 2015, www.preceptaustin.org /romans_12_notes#12:13.

28. Henri J. M. Nouwen, *Reaching Out: The Three Movements of the Spiritual Life* (New York: Image, 1986), 66.

29. Nouwen, *Reaching Out,* 67.

30. Ronald Rolheiser, *Sacred Fire: A Vision for a Deeper Human and Christian Maturity* (New York: Image, 2014), 260.

31. Rosaria Champagne Butterfield, *The Gospel Comes with a House Key: Practicing Radically Ordinary Hospitality in Our Post-Christian World* (Wheaton, Ill.: Crossway, 2018), 11.

32. "Almost Half of Practicing Christian Millennials Say Evangelism Is Wrong," Barna, February 5,

2019, www.barna.com/research/millennials-oppose-evangelism.

33. Mark 1v15.

34. Romans 10v9; Philippians 2v11; 1 Corinthians 12v3.

35. Alpha.org.

36. Daniel A. Cox, "The State of American Friendship: Change, Challenge, and Loss," Survey Center on American Life, June 18, 2021, www.americansurveycenter.org/research/the-state-of-american-friendship-change-challenges-and-loss.

37. Chris Jackson and Negar Ballard, "Over Half of Americans Report Feeling Like No One Knows Them Well," Ipsos, May 1, 2018, www.ipsos.com/en-us/news-polls/us-loneliness-index-report.

38. Acts 1v8.

39. Mortimer Arias, *Announcing the Reign of God: Evangelization and the Subversive Memory of Jesus* (Eugene, Ore.: Wipf and Stock, 2001), 43.

40. 1 John 1v2, NKJV.

41. I highly recommend his book *Power Healing*.

42. 1 Peter 2v12.

43. Henry George Liddell and Robert Scott, comps., *A Greek-English Lexicon,* 9th ed., with rev. supplement (Oxford: Clarendon Press, 1996).

44. Dallas Willard, *The Spirit of the Disciplines: Understanding How God Changes Lives* (San Francisco: HarperSanFrancisco, 1991), 247.

45. *Strong's Definitions,* s.v. "*martys,*" Blue Letter Bible, www.blueletterbible.org/lexicon/g3144/niv/mgnt/0-1.

46. Philippians 3v8.

47. 1 Thessalonians 5v19.

48. Frank Charles Laubach, *Letters by a Modern Mystic* (London: Society for Promoting Christian Knowledge, 2011), 34.

49. Luke 19v9.

50. Jürgen Moltmann, *The Way of Jesus Christ: Christology in Messianic Dimensions* (Minneapolis: Fortress, 1993), 98–99.

51. Matthew 4v24, NLT.

52. Acts 5v15.

53. Acts 19v11–12.

54. James 5v16.

55. My favorite two books on healing are *Healing* by Dr. Francis McNutt and *Power Healing* by John Wimber.

56. 1 John 3v8, ESV. A couple of recommendations for books on deliverance are *Deliverance* by Jon Thompson and *The Believer's Guide to Spiritual Warfare* by Tom White.

57. To hear my wife T's story, listen to the podcast we did together:

"Fasting 02: To Grow in Holiness" on the *Rule of Life* podcast from Practicing the Way.

58. John 4v18, AMP.

59. John 9v3.

60. See Tim Keller's accessible and incredibly helpful overview of Alasdair MacIntyre's book *Whose Justice? Which Rationality?* in the article "A Biblical Critique of Secular Justice and Critical Theory," *Life in the Gospel.* Dr. Keller, you are deeply missed.

61. This is from a handout he gave us students in a seminary class.

62. Bishop Kallistos Ware, *The Orthodox Way,* rev. ed. (Crestwood, N.Y.: St. Vladimir's Seminary, 1995), 141.

63. Mark 16v15.

64. My paraphrase of John 5v19.

65. 1 Corinthians 12v27.

66. Mark Etling, "Christ Has No Body on Earth but Yours," *National Catholic Reporter,* January 21, 2020.

67. Thomas Raymond Kelly, *A Testament of Devotion* (San Francisco: HarperSanFrancisco, 1992), 64–65.

68. Kelly, *A Testament of Devotion,* 35.

69. 1 Corinthians 3v5.

70. Tony Evans, *Tony Evans Speaks Out on Fasting* (Chicago: Moody, 2000), 42.

71. Kahlil Gibran, "On Work," Poets.org, https://poets.org/poem/work-4.

72. Martin Luther King Jr., "Facing the Challenge of a New Age" (speech, First Annual Institute on Nonviolence and Social Change, Montgomery, Alabama, December 3, 1956), in *The Papers of Martin Luther King Jr.,* vol. 3, *Birth of a New Age, December 1955—December 1956,* ed. Clayborne Carson et al. (Berkeley, Calif.: University of California Press, 1997).

73. Matthew 5v16.

74. Hebrews 4v15.

How? A Rule of Life

1. Peter Scazzero, *Emotionally Healthy Spirituality,* updated ed. (Grand Rapids, Mich.: Zondervan, 2017), 191.

2. John Ortberg, *Soul Keeping: Caring for the Most Important Part of You* (Grand Rapids, Mich.: Zondervan, 2014), 89.

3. *Online Etymology Dictionary,* s.v. "rule," www.etymonline.com/word/rule.

4. Rich Villodas, *The Deeply Formed Life: Five Transformative Values to Root Us in the Way of Jesus* (Colorado Springs: WaterBrook, 2020), 217–18.

5. 1 Corinthians 4v17.

6. David Brooks, *The Second Mountain: The Quest for a Moral Life* (New York: Random House, 2020), xviii.

7. Dietrich Bonhoeffer, quoted in Ronald Rolheiser, *Our One Great Act of Fidelity* (New York: Doubleday, 2011), 78. It was in a letter he wrote to his niece on her wedding day, as he was imprisoned by the Gestapo. Shortly later, he was martyred.

8. See www.practicingtheway.org/spiritualhealthreflection.

9. A summary of thoughts from Francis Spufford, *Unapologetic: Why, Despite Everything, Christianity Can Still Make Surprising Emotional Sense* (New York: HarperOne, 2013).

10. Annie Dillard, *The Writing Life* (New York: Harper Perennial, 2013), 32.

11. "Preamble," A Rule of Life for Redemptive Entrepreneurs, https://rule.praxislabs.org/preamble. See the Rule Andy and others developed for Praxis: https://rule.praxislabs.org.

12. Guess what? They are still alive!

13. I find it helpful to fully delete the app each week. Just saying.

14. See the entire Rule at https://rule.praxislabs.org/the-rule-in-one-page.

15. Marcel Schwantes, "Steve Jobs's Advice on the Only 4 Times You Should Say No Is Brilliant," *Inc.,* January 31, 2018, www.inc.com/marcel-schwantes/first-90-days-steve-jobs-advice-on-the-only-4-times-you-should-say-no.html.

16. Romans 7v19.

17. T. S. Eliot, "Burnt Norton," in *Four Quartets* (New York: Harcourt, Brace, 1943), 17.

18. Two books that do an excellent job explaining how the algorithms utilize fear and anger are *Ten Reasons for Deleting Your Social Media Accounts Right Now* by Jaron Lanier and *Stolen Focus* by Johann Hari.

19. Philippians 3v14.

20. Margaret Guenther, *Toward Holy Ground: Spiritual Directions for the Second Half of Life* (Lanham, Md.: Cowley, 1995), 66.

21. Craig Dykstra, *Growing in the Life of Faith,* 2nd ed. (London: Westminster John Knox, 2005), 67.

22. I shy away from this language for two simple (and non-emotionally loaded) reasons: (1) For many people, *spiritual* means disembodied (which is the Platonic meaning, not the Scriptural one, but sadly is the most common usage in the Western church), but the practices are all about how you get Jesus' vision from your mind into your body. For the New Testament writers, your body is the focal point of your relationship to God (his "temple"), and what you do with it matters. And (2) *discipline* is a great word—I love it—but it has negative connotations in our anti-rule culture. Since *spiritual disciplines* isn't language used by Scripture and *practice* is, I prefer to call them the practices of Jesus whenever I can.

23. Ruth Haley Barton, *Sacred Rhythms: Arranging Our Lives for Spiritual Transformation* (Downers Grove, Ill.: IVP Books, 2006).

24. Matthew 11v28–30, MSG.

25. "Means of Grace," Ligonier Ministries, June 26, 2012, www.ligonier.org/learn/devotionals/means-of-grace.

26. Richard Plass and James Cofield, *The Relational Soul: Moving from False Self to Deep Connection* (Downers Grove, Ill.: IVP Books, 2014), 134.

27. To clarify, not because of those three practices but in spite of them.

28. Richard J. Foster, *Celebration of Discipline: The Path to Spiritual Growth,* 20th anniv. ed. (San Francisco: HarperSanFrancisco, 1998), 2.

29. John Ortberg, *The Life You've Always Wanted: Spiritual Disciplines for Ordinary People* (Grand Rapids, Mich.: Zondervan, 2002), 46.

30. In the Sermon on the Mount, Matthew 6v1–18.

31. Grace, for Paul, is far more than just "unmerited favor," as I was taught in my younger years. It's a kind of synonym for the Spirit of God giving us the capacity to be and do what we can never be or do on our own.

32. Dallas Willard, *The Spirit of the Disciplines: Understanding How God Changes Lives* (San Francisco: HarperSanFrancisco, 1991), 68.

33. Philippians 2v13, NLT.

34. Trivia: All of my immediate family named their dogs after Star Wars' characters—Kylo (as in Ren), Jango (as in Fett), Obi (as in Wan Kenobi) and Trooper (as in Storm . . .). Naturally, we had to join in.

35. M. Robert Mulholland Jr., *Invitation to a Journey: A Road Map for Spiritual Formation,* expanded ed. (Downers Grove, Ill.: IVP Books, 2016), 90.

36. Other core aspects of spiritual formation include healing from memories (especially trauma), offering forgiveness to those who have hurt you, breaking unhealthy patterns from your family of origin, receiving deliverance, caring for the body, living in community, letting suffering liberate you from attachments, and more . . .

37. Nan Fink, *Stranger in the Midst: A Memoir of Spiritual Discovery* (New York: BasicBooks, 1997), 96.

38. Henri Nouwen, *The Spiritual Life: Eight Essential Titles by Henri Nouwen* (New York: HarperOne, 2016), 24.

39. James A. Connor, *Silent Fire: Bringing the Spirituality of Silence to Everyday Life* (New York: Crown, 2002), 203.

40. "An Exercise in Wonder," Christian History Institute, https://christianhistoryinstitute.org/magazine/article/an-exercise-in-wonder.

41. Luke 5v16.

42. This is my adaptation of Mark E. Thibodeaux, *Armchair Mystic: How Contemplative Prayer Can Lead You Closer to God* (Cincinnati, Ohio: Franciscan Media, 2019).

43. Ronald Rolheiser, *Prayer: Our Deepest Longing* (Cincinnati, Ohio: Franciscan Media, 2013), viii.

44. John 4v32.

45. Romans 12v2.

46. 1 Corinthians 2v16.

47. I simply cannot recommend more strongly that you follow everything from the BibleProject: https://bibleproject.com.

48. This is from his upcoming book *Steps: A Guide to Transforming Your Life When Willpower Isn't Enough.*

49. John 3v16; 14v16, 26.

50. Ronald Rolheiser, *Sacred Fire: A Vision for a Deeper Human and Christian Maturity* (New York: Image, 2014), 260.

51. See Acts 20v35.

52. Matthew 20v28.

53. John 13v15, 17.

54. Mark 16v15.

55. Rosaria Champagne Butterfield, *The Gospel Comes with a House Key: Practicing Radically Ordinary Hospitality in Our Post-Christian World* (Wheaton, Ill.: Crossway, 2018).

56. This is a saying from my friend Pete Greig and the crew at 24/7.

57. Margaret Guenther, *At Home in the World: A Rule of Life for the Rest of Us* (New York: Seabury, 2006), 178.

58. Dallas Willard, *The Divine Conspiracy: Rediscovering Our Hidden Life in God,* 20th anniv. ed. (New York: HarperOne, 2018), 348.

59. BJ Fogg, *Tiny Habits: The Small Changes That Change Everything* (New York: Houghton Mifflin Harcourt, 2020).

60. Gary Thomas, *Sacred Pathways: Discover Your Soul's Path to God,* rev. ed. (Grand Rapids, Mich.: Zondervan, 2010), 17, 36.

61. Thomas, *Sacred Pathways,* chaps. 3–11.

62. You simply *must* go read *Domestic Monastery* by Ronald Rolheiser if you are a young parent. Don't worry; it's short.

63. Tish Harrison Warren, *Liturgy of the Ordinary: Sacred Practices in Everyday Life* (Downers Grove, Ill.: IVP Books, 2016), 99.

64. Much more could be said about this. I would invite you to listen to two teachings on the subject I did here: www.practicingtheway.org /practices/naming.

65. To my fellow pastors: My dream is that the churches of the future (like the churches of the past) will organize around a Rule of Life—a way of being together, contextualized for their time, their place, and their people. It can happen. Would you consider this?

66. Nathan Campbell, "Educating Loves: A Morning in Brisbane with James K. A. Smith," St. Eutychus, https://st-eutychus.com/2016 /educating-loves-a-morning-in -brisbane-with-james-ka-smith.

67. G. K. Chesterton, *Orthodoxy* (Peabody, Mass.: Hendrickson, 2006), 55.

68. Ken Shigematsu, *God in My Everything: How an Ancient Rhythm Helps Busy People Enjoy God* (Grand Rapids, Mich.: Zondervan, 2013), 20.

69. Greg Peters, *The Monkhood of All Believers: The Monastic Foundation of Christian Spirituality* (Ada, Mich.: Baker, 2018).

70. Walter H. Capps, *The Monastic Impulse* (New York: Crossroad, 1983).

71. Jerome, quoted in Laurie Guy, *Introducing Early Christianity: A Topical Survey of Its Life, Beliefs and Practices* (Downers Grove, Ill.: InterVarsity, 2004), 139.

72. Benedict, *The Rule of St. Benedict in English,* ed. Timothy Fry (Collegeville, Minn.: Liturgical Press, 2019), 18–19.

Take up your cross

1. Mark Scandrette, *Practicing the Way of Jesus: Life Together in the King-*

dom of Love (Downers Grove, Ill.: IVP Books, 2011), 89.

2. Both stories are found in Luke 9v59–61.

3. Don't give the "right" answer but the honest one. Faking it won't help you in the least. It could be that, for you, the spiritual journey begins not with wanting to follow Jesus but with wanting *to want* to follow Jesus. Okay, start there. Take the next step: Pray *that* to Jesus.

4. Luke 9v23.

5. Dietrich Bonhoeffer, *The Cost of Discipleship* (New York: Touchstone, 1995), 89.

6. John 15v20.

7. A saying first attributed to Tertullian in the second century.

8. Jaroslav Pelikan, *The Shape of Death: Life, Death and Immortality in the Early Fathers* (Nashville, Tenn.: Abingdon, 1961), 55.

9. Thank you to Kevin Jenkins for this. (He is chairman of the board for Practicing the Way and the former CEO of World Vision.)

10. John 14v15, ESV.

11. Matthew 28v20.

12. Romans 7v24, ESV.

13. Psalm 73v26.

14. See his book *Will and Spirit: A Contemplative Psychology* (New York: HarperOne, 2009), chap. 1.

15. Thomas Keating, *Open Mind, Open Heart: The Contemplative Dimension of the Gospel,* 20th anniv. ed. (London: Bloomsbury Continuum, 2006), 65.

16. Luke 22v42.

17. Philippians 4v7; 1 Peter 1v8, ESV.

18. Mark 8v35.

19. In the ancient world, there were no banks, so a person of means would often bury their money or gold somewhere secret. But if they died, the knowledge of where to find it died with them. This is a plausible story out of first-century life.

20. Elisabeth Elliott, ed., *The Journals of Jim Elliott* (Grand Rapids, Mich.: Revell, 2002), 174.

21. Johann Wolfgang von Goethe, "The Holy Longing," trans. Robert Bly, York University, www.yorku .ca/lfoster/documents/The_Holy _Longing_Goethe.htm.

22. Tito Colliander, *Way of the Ascetics: The Ancient Tradition of Discipline and Inner Growth,* trans. Katherine Ferré (San Francisco: Harper and Row, 1982), 54.

23. Frank Charles Laubach, *Letters by a Modern Mystic* (London: Society for Promoting Christian Knowledge, 2011), 25.

24. Gregory of Nyssa, "Perfection Is Friendship with God," Renovaré, January 2023, https://renovare.org/articles/perfection-is-friendship-with-god.

25. This story is told by Gary Moon, who was a mentee of Dallas, in his book *Apprenticeship with Jesus: Learning to Live Like the Master* (Grand Rapids, Mich.: Baker, 2009), 241.

26. Thomas R. Kelly, *A Testament of Devotion* (San Francisco: HarperSan Francisco, 1992), 29.

Extras

1. Revelation 4v11.

About Practicing the Way

Practicing the Way is a nonprofit that creates spiritual formation resources for churches and small groups learning how to become apprentices of the Way of Jesus.

We believe one of the greatest needs of our time is for people to discover how to become lifelong disciples of Jesus. To that end, we help people learn how to be with Jesus, become like him, and do as he did through the practices and rhythms he and his earliest followers lived by.

All of our downloadable ministry resources are available at no cost, thanks to the generosity of The Circle, a group of monthly givers from around the world who partner with us to see formation integrated into the church at large.

To learn more, visit practicingtheway.org.

Bulk Book Orders

To order a bulk quantity of *Practicing the Way* for your staff, small group leaders, and church attendees, use the QR code on this page to contact Penguin Random House Christian sales or email your bulk order inquiry to churches@penguinrandomhouse.com with *Practicing the Way* in the subject line.

johnmarkcomer.com/bulk-discount

John Mark Comer is a teacher, a writer, and the founder of Practicing the Way.

After serving as the pastor for teaching and vision at Bridgetown Church in Portland, Oregon, for nearly two decades, John Mark and his family now reside in Los Angeles, where he serves as a teacher in residence at Vintage Church LA.

He is the *New York Times* bestselling author of seven books, including international bestseller *The Ruthless Elimination of Hurry.* His podcasts, *John Mark Comer Teachings* and *Rule of Life,* have been ranked on top religion and spirituality podcast charts in the US and UK.

Podcast resources also available

Through roundtable discussions, guest interviews, and listener stories, this podcast offers practical wisdom for arranging everyday life around being with and becoming like Jesus. Each season, you'll learn more about building a Rule of Life as you practice the Way of Jesus.

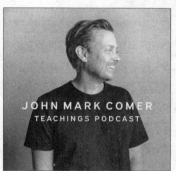

Through his teachings from Bridgetown Church in Portland, Oregon, John Mark Comer provides insight into how you can practice the Way of Jesus in today's complex, secular world in this podcast by Practicing the Way.

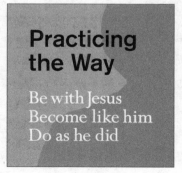

John Mark Comer, joined by Tyler Staton, dives deeper into the themes discussed in Practicing the Way. Together, they lay out a vision of apprenticeship to Jesus, explaining how transformation is possible in our cultural moment of hurry and digital distraction.

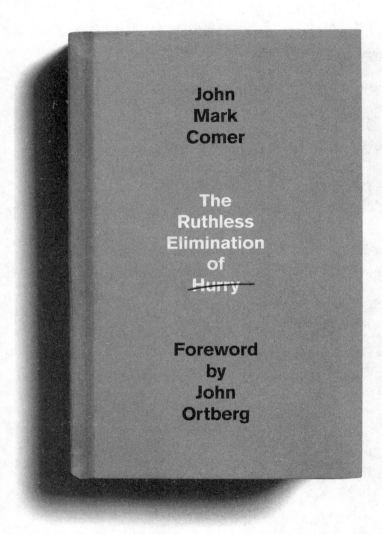

National Bestseller, with More Than Half a Million Copies Sold

John
Mark
Comer

The
Ruthless
Elimination
of
Hurry

Foreword
by
John
Ortberg

"Pastor John Mark Comer maps the road to peace and calm."
— *Publishers Weekly*

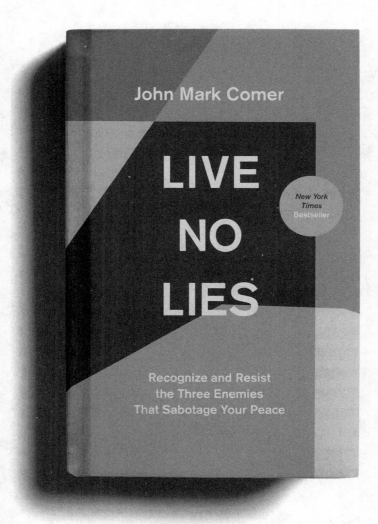

John Mark Comer

LIVE
NO
LIES

New York Times Bestseller

Recognize and Resist
the Three Enemies
That Sabotage Your Peace

About the Type

This book was set in Perpetua, a typeface designed by the English artist Eric Gill (1882–1940), and cut by the Monotype Corporation between 1928 and 1930. Originally used for both fine book printing and inscribing names and sayings onto monuments in England, it was named after the early Christian martyr Perpetua, who gave her life rather than renounce her faith in Jesus. The italic was originally named Felicity after Perpetua's companion of the same name. Their courage and inner peace in the face of death inspired untold thousands of early Christians to stay true to the Way of Jesus in the coming centuries of persecution, and their story continues to inspire us today.